بسم الله الرحمن الرحيم

THE 8 GATES OF JANNAH

A COLLECTION OF PROPHETIC NARRATIONS PERTAINING TO THE GATES OF JANNAH

SHAYKH DR. ALI AHMED

QUILLSPIRE

QUILLSPIRE

The 8 Gates of Jannah

A Collection of Prophetic Narrations Pertaining to the Gates of Jannah

---

For more information or permission requests, contact:

Quillspire Ltd

Email: contact@quillspire.com

Website: www.quillspire.com

ISBN: 9781739521516

First Edition

A Dedication

وَٱلَّذِينَ ءَامَنُوا۟ وَٱتَّبَعَتْهُمْ ذُرِّيَّتُهُم بِإِيمَـٰنٍ أَلْحَقْنَا بِهِمْ ذُرِّيَّتَهُمْ وَمَآ أَلَتْنَـٰهُم مِّنْ عَمَلِهِم مِّن شَىْءٍ ۚ كُلُّ ٱمْرِئٍۭ بِمَا كَسَبَ رَهِينٌ ﴿٢١﴾

"Those who believed and whose descendants followed them in faith – We will join with them their descendants, and We will not deprive them of anything of their deeds. Every person, for what he earned, is retained." (*al-Ṭūr*, 52:21)

To my parents: I make *duʿā* for you in every *sajdah* and ask Allah to enter me into *Jannah* through the Gate of Parents.

Honorifics Key

For the Divine

Symbol	Arabic	Translation
﷾	سُبْحَانَهُ وَتَعَالَىٰ	Hallowed and exalted be He
﵎	تَبَارَكَ وَتَعَالَىٰ	Blessed and exalted be He
جل وعلا	جَلَّ وَعَلَا	Majestic and exalted be He
﷿	عَزَّ وَجَلَّ	Mighty and majestic be He
ﷻ	جَلَّ جَلَالُهُ	Awesome be His majesty

Prayers of *Salām*

Symbol	Arabic	Translation
ﷺ	صَلَّى ٱللهُ عَلَيْهِ وَسَلَّمَ	Allah confer blessing and peace upon him
﵊	عَلَيْهِ ٱلصَّلَاةُ وَٱلسَّلَامُ	Upon him be blessing and peace
﵇	عَلَيْهِ ٱلسَّلَامُ	Upon him be peace
﵍	عَلَيْهَا ٱلسَّلَامُ	Upon her be peace
﵉	عَلَيْهِمَا ٱلسَّلَامُ	Upon them (dual) be peace
﵈	عَلَيْهِمُ ٱلسَّلَامُ	Upon them be peace

Prayers of *Riḍā*

Symbol	Arabic	Translation
﵁	رَضِيَ ٱللّٰهُ عَنْهُ	Allah be pleased with him
﵂	رَضِيَ ٱللّٰهُ عَنْهَا	Allah be pleased with her
﵄	رَضِيَ ٱللّٰهُ عَنْهُمَا	Allah be pleased with them (dual)
﵅	رَضِيَ ٱللّٰهُ عَنْهُمْ	Allah be pleased with them
﵃	رَضِيَ ٱللّٰهُ عَنْهُنَّ	Allah be pleased with them (fem)

Prayers of *Raḥmah*

Symbol	Arabic	Translation
﵀	رَحِمَهُ ٱللّٰهُ	Allah have mercy on him
﵀	رَحِمَهَا ٱللّٰهُ	Allah have mercy on her
﵀	رَحِمَهُمَا ٱللّٰهُ	Allah have mercy on them (dual)
﵀	رَحِمَهُمْ ٱللّٰهُ	Allah have mercy on them
﵀	رَحِمَهُنَّ ٱللّٰهُ	Allah have mercy on them (fem)

CONTENTS

Foreword

بِسْمِ اللّٰهِ وَالْحَمْدُ لِلّٰهِ

وَالصَّلَاةُ وَالسَّلَامُ عَلَى رَسُولِ اللّٰهِ

وَعَلَى آلِهِ وَصَحْبِهِ وَمَن وَالَاه

أَمَّا بَعدُ

Praise be to Allah, the Lord of the Worlds. May His blessings and peace be upon the Messenger of Allah (ﷺ), as well as his family, his companions, and all his followers.

I had a look at the work of our dear brother Sh. Ali Ahmed which he titled "The 8 Gates of *Jannah*", and I found it to be a beautiful collection of *āyāt*, *aḥādīth*, and *āthār* relating to the Gates of *Jannah*. The book acts as a useful resource for those seeking information on the topic. It can also be used by community imams for their sermons and families for their circles of remembrance.

The book does not offer commentary (*sharḥ*) on the quoted passages. It aims to relate the content in clear English for readers to immediately benefit from the guidance and wisdom held within it. Perhaps explanations of the narrations quoted is something to consider for future renditions.

May Allah place *barakah* in this work, and may He make us among those who will be allowed to enter *Jannah* from whichever gate they desire. *Āmīn.*

Shaykh Dr. Haitham al-Haddad

Introduction

الحمَدُ لله رَبِّ العَالَمِين

وَالصَّلاةُ وَالسَّلاَمُ عَلى رَسُولِ الله

وَعَلى آلِهِ وَصَحبِه أَجمَعِين

أَمَّا بَعدُ

All praises are due to Allah, the Lord of the Universe, and may His blessings and peace be upon the Messenger of Allah (ﷺ), his family, and his companions.

Every human being wants Paradise. Some haplessly seek it in this world at the expense of their Hereafter, while others seek only the Garden which Allah promised His obedient slaves. The Qur'an and the Sunnah teach us to wish and work for that which is eternal and everlasting:

بَلْ تُؤْثِرُونَ ٱلْحَيَوٰةَ ٱلدُّنْيَا ﴿١٦﴾ وَٱلْـَٔاخِرَةُ خَيْرٌ وَأَبْقَىٰٓ ﴿١٧﴾

"But you prefer the worldly life, while the Hereafter is better and more lasting." (*al-Aʿlā*, 87:16-17)

إِنَّ ٱلَّذِينَ ءَامَنُوا۟ وَعَمِلُوا۟ ٱلصَّـٰلِحَـٰتِ كَانَتْ لَهُمْ جَنَّـٰتُ ٱلْفِرْدَوْسِ نُزُلًا ﴿١٠٧﴾ خَـٰلِدِينَ فِيهَا لَا يَبْغُونَ عَنْهَا حِوَلًا ﴿١٠٨﴾

"Indeed, those who have believed and done righteous deeds – they will have the Gardens of Paradise as a lodging, wherein they will abide eternally. They will not desire from it any transfer." (*al-Kahf*, 18:107-108)

When it comes to *Jannah*, we **must** want it, desire it, beggingly ask Allah for it, and expend all efforts to reach it. As believers, we should have high hopes and lofty ambitions for *Jannah* – that Allah gives us the best and the highest part of it. We should be thinking and pondering about which gate of *Jannah* we want to enter through. When we have this mindset, the deeds (e.g., prayer and fasting) that are specific to that gate (e.g., the

Gate of Ṣalāh and al-Rayyān), will be performed out of love, with ease, and without any hesitation or burden.

For this reason, I have collected some of the prophetic narrations pertaining to the Eight Gates of *Jannah* in this book. After the pleasure of Allah, it is collated with multiple goals and intentions in mind: so that it may be read together as a family, that *masjid* imams may use it in their weekly lessons with their congregants, that it reorients and gives renewed focus to the youth, and for the reader to simply discover which gate of *Jannah* they aspire to enter through and consequently work towards. I have abstained from making my own commentary, as most of these reports are self-explanatory and straightforward. The book is not written as a rigorous, academic discussion of scholarly positions on the subject. Rather, its aim is to edify its readers and rejuvenate their zeal to seeking the everlasting bliss Allah has promised us.

Though the book is titled "The 8 Gates of *Jannah*", readers will notice that there are 11 gates mentioned altogether. This is because scholars are in agreement over four out of the eight gates since there are four clearly mentioned together in a *ḥadīth*. However, scholars have differed over the names of the remaining four. There are other opinions on the remaining four gates in addition to what is mentioned in the book. For the purposes of brevity, and due to what I thought the majority of the *Ummah* is in need of, I capped it at 11 total. Studious readers are invited to research the other names of the Gates of *Jannah* not mentioned in this book.

I ask Allah through His beautiful names that He grants us all and our families the highest level of *Jannat al-Firdaws*, in the company of the prophets, the truthful ones, the martyrs, and the righteous, and excellent are those as companions. *Āmīn*!

Shaykh Dr. Ali Ahmed

Āyāt Pertaining to the Gates of Jannah

إِنَّ ٱلَّذِينَ كَذَّبُوا۟ بِـَٔايَـٰتِنَا وَٱسْتَكْبَرُوا۟ عَنْهَا لَا تُفَتَّحُ لَهُمْ أَبْوَٰبُ ٱلسَّمَآءِ وَلَا يَدْخُلُونَ ٱلْجَنَّةَ حَتَّىٰ يَلِجَ ٱلْجَمَلُ فِى سَمِّ ٱلْخِيَاطِ ۚ وَكَذَٰلِكَ نَجْزِى ٱلْمُجْرِمِينَ ﴿٤٠﴾

"Indeed, those who deny Our verses and are arrogant toward them - the Gates of Heaven will not be opened for them, nor will they enter *Jannah* until a camel enters into the eye of a needle (i.e., never). And thus do We recompense the criminals." (*al-Aʿrāf*, 7:40)

وَسِيقَ ٱلَّذِينَ ٱتَّقَوْا۟ رَبَّهُمْ إِلَى ٱلْجَنَّةِ زُمَرًا ۖ حَتَّىٰٓ إِذَا جَآءُوهَا وَفُتِحَتْ أَبْوَٰبُهَا وَقَالَ لَهُمْ خَزَنَتُهَا سَلَـٰمٌ عَلَيْكُمْ طِبْتُمْ فَٱدْخُلُوهَا خَـٰلِدِينَ ﴿٧٣﴾

"And those who kept their duty to their Lord will be led to *Jannah* in groups, till, when they reach it, its gates will be opened (before their arrival for their reception) and its keepers will say: '*Salāmun ʿAlaykum* (peace be upon you)! You have done well, so enter here to abide therein.' " (*al-Zumar*, 39:73)

جَنَّـٰتُ عَدْنٍ يَدْخُلُونَهَا وَمَن صَلَحَ مِنْ ءَابَآئِهِمْ وَأَزْوَٰجِهِمْ وَذُرِّيَّـٰتِهِمْ ۖ وَٱلْمَلَـٰٓئِكَةُ يَدْخُلُونَ عَلَيْهِم مِّن كُلِّ بَابٍ ﴿٢٣﴾ سَلَـٰمٌ عَلَيْكُم بِمَا صَبَرْتُمْ ۚ فَنِعْمَ عُقْبَى ٱلدَّارِ ﴿٢٤﴾

"Gardens of perpetual residence; they will enter them with whoever was righteous among their forefathers, their spouses and their descendants. And the angels will enter upon them from every gate, [saying]: 'Peace be upon you for what you patiently endured. And excellent is the final home.' " (*al-Raʿd*, 13:23-24)

جَنَّـٰتِ عَدْنٍ مُّفَتَّحَةً لَّهُمُ ٱلْأَبْوَٰبُ ﴿٥٠﴾ مُتَّكِـِٔينَ فِيهَا يَدْعُونَ فِيهَا بِفَـٰكِهَةٍ كَثِيرَةٍ وَشَرَابٍ ﴿٥١﴾

"Gardens of perpetual residence, whose doors will be opened to them. Reclining within them, they will call therein for abundant fruit and drink." (*Ṣād*, 38:50-51)

Ḥadīth Pertaining to Some Gates of Jannah

Abū Hurayrah (رضي الله عنه) narrates that the Prophet (ﷺ) said:

مَنْ أَنْفَقَ زَوْجَيْنِ فِي سَبِيلِ اللَّهِ نُودِيَ مِنْ أَبْوَابِ الْجَنَّةِ يَا عَبْدَ اللَّهِ هَذَا خَيْرٌ فَمَنْ كَانَ مِنْ أَهْلِ الصَّلَاةِ دُعِيَ مِنْ بَابِ الصَّلَاةِ وَمَنْ كَانَ مِنْ أَهْلِ الْجِهَادِ دُعِيَ مِنْ بَابِ الْجِهَادِ وَمَنْ كَانَ مِنْ أَهْلِ الصِّيَامِ دُعِيَ مِنْ بَابِ الرَّيَّانِ وَمَنْ كَانَ مِنْ أَهْلِ الصَّدَقَةِ دُعِيَ مِنْ بَابِ الصَّدَقَةِ فَقَالَ أَبُو بَكْرٍ رَضِيَ اللَّهُ عَنْهُ بِأَبِي أَنْتَ وَأُمِّي يَا رَسُولَ اللَّهِ مَا عَلَى مَنْ دُعِيَ مِنْ تِلْكَ الْأَبْوَابِ مِنْ ضَرُورَةٍ فَهَلْ يُدْعَى أَحَدٌ مِنْ تِلْكَ الْأَبْوَابِ كُلِّهَا قَالَ نَعَمْ وَأَرْجُو أَنْ تَكُونَ مِنْهُمْ

" 'Anyone who spends a pair (2 dinars, 2 dirhams, or any 2 things, or is habitual in spending) in the way of Allah will be called from all the Gates of *Jannah*: 'O servant of Allah, this is good!' The people of prayer will be called from the Gate of Prayer, the people of jihad will be called from the Gate of Jihad, the people of fasting will be called from the Gate of *al-Rayyān*, and the people of charity will be called from the Gate of Charity.' Abū Bakr (رضي الله عنه) said, 'One who is called from all those gates would need nothing. Will anyone be called from all those gates, O Messenger of Allah?' The Prophet (ﷺ) said, 'Yes, and I hope you will be among them, O Abū Bakr.' " (*Ṣaḥīḥ al-Bukhārī* 3666, *Ṣaḥīḥ Muslim* 1027)

When Do the Gates of Jannah Open?

1. *In Ramaḍān*

Abū Hurayrah (رضي الله عنه) reported: The Messenger of Allah (ﷺ) said:

إِذَا كَانَ أَوَّلُ لَيْلَةٍ مِنْ شَهْرِ رَمَضَانَ صُفِّدَتْ الشَّيَاطِينُ وَمَرَدَةُ الْجِنِّ وَغُلِّقَتْ أَبْوَابُ النَّارِ فَلَمْ يُفْتَحْ مِنْهَا بَابٌ وَفُتِّحَتْ أَبْوَابُ الْجَنَّةِ فَلَمْ يُغْلَقْ مِنْهَا بَابٌ وَيُنَادِي مُنَادٍ يَا بَاغِيَ الْخَيْرِ أَقْبِلْ وَيَا بَاغِيَ الشَّرِّ أَقْصِرْ وَلِلَّهِ عُتَقَاءُ مِنْ النَّارِ وَذَلِكَ كُلُّ لَيْلَةٍ

"On the first night of the month of *Ramaḍān*, the devils are chained, the jinn are restrained, and the gates of *Jahannam* are closed and none of its gates are opened. The Gates of *Jannah* are opened and none of its gates are closed. A caller announces: 'O seeker of good, come near! O seeker of evil, stop short!' Allah will save people from *Jahannam* and that is during every night of *Ramaḍān*." (*Sunan al-Tirmidhī* 682, *Ṣaḥīḥ* according to al-Albānī)

2. *Every Monday and Thursday*

Abū Hurayrah (رضي الله عنه) reported: The Messenger of Allah (ﷺ) said:

تُفْتَحُ أَبْوَابُ الْجَنَّةِ يَوْمَ الْإِثْنَيْنِ، وَيَوْمَ الْخَمِيسِ، فَيُغْفَرُ لِكُلِّ عَبْدٍ لَا يُشْرِكُ بِاللهِ شَيْئًا، إِلَّا رَجُلًا كَانَتْ بَيْنَهُ وَبَيْنَ أَخِيهِ شَحْنَاءُ، فَيُقَالُ: أَنْظِرُوا هَذَيْنِ حَتَّى يَصْطَلِحَا، أَنْظِرُوا هَذَيْنِ حَتَّى يَصْطَلِحَا، أَنْظِرُوا هَذَيْنِ حَتَّى يَصْطَلِحَا

قالَ في تُحفة الأَحوَذي شَرح سُنَن التِّرمِذي: قَولُه: (تُفْتَحُ أبْوابُ الجَنَّةِ يَومَ الإثْنَينِ والخَميس) أي لِكَثرةِ الرَّحمةِ النَّازِلَة فيهِما الباعِثَةِ عَلى الغُفْران

"The Gates of *Jannah* are opened on Monday and Thursday. Allah forgives every servant who does not associate anything with Him, except a man with enmity between himself and his brother. It will be said: 'Delay these two until they reconcile, delay these two until they reconcile, delay these two until they reconcile.' " (*Ṣaḥīḥ Muslim* 2565, and *Sunan al-Tirmidhī* 2023)

What is meant by, "the Gates of *Jannah* are opened on Monday and Thursday", is the abundance of mercy and forgiveness that descends on these two days. (*Tuḥfat al-Aḥwadhī Sharḥ Sunan al-Tirmidhī, Ḥadīth* 2023)

3. *After making wuḍūʾ*

ʿUmar ibn al-Khaṭṭāb (ﷺ) reported: The Messenger of Allah (ﷺ) said:

مَنْ تَوَضَّأَ فَأَحْسَنَ الْوُضُوءَ ثُمَّ قَالَ أَشْهَدُ أَنْ لَا إِلَهَ إِلَّا اللَّهُ وَحْدَهُ لَا شَرِيكَ لَهُ وَأَشْهَدُ أَنَّ مُحَمَّدًا عَبْدُهُ وَرَسُولُهُ اللَّهُمَّ اجْعَلْنِي مِنْ التَّوَّابِينَ وَاجْعَلْنِي مِنْ الْمُتَطَهِّرِينَ فُتِحَتْ لَهُ ثَمَانِيَةُ أَبْوَابِ الْجَنَّةِ يَدْخُلُ مِنْ أَيِّهَا شَاءَ

"Whoever performs ablution (*wuḍūʾ*) in the best manner and he says: 'I bear witness that there is no god but Allah alone, without any partners, and I bear witness that Muhammad is His servant and His messenger. O Allah, make me among the repentant and make me among those who purify themselves,' then the Eight Gates of *Jannah* will be opened for him and he may enter through whichever he wishes." (*Sunan al-Tirmidhī* 55, Weak – *iḍṭirāb* according to Abū ʿĪsā al-Tirmidhī, but *Ṣaḥīḥ* according al-Albānī in *Ṣaḥīḥ al-Jāmiʿ* 6167)

ʿUqbah ibn ʿĀmir (ﷺ) reported:

"We were entrusted with the task of tending the camels. On my turn when I came back in the evening after grazing them in the pastures, I found Allah's Messenger (ﷺ) standing and addressing the people. I heard these words of his:

مَا مِنْ مُسْلِمٍ يَتَوَضَّأُ فَيُحْسِنُ وُضُوءَهُ ثُمَّ يَقُومُ فَيُصَلِّي رَكْعَتَيْنِ مُقْبِلٌ عَلَيْهِمَا بِقَلْبِهِ وَوَجْهِهِ إِلَّا

وَجَبَتْ لَهُ الْجَنَّةُ

'There is no *muslim* who performs ablution properly, then gets up and offers two *rakaʿāt* turning to them wholeheartedly, except that *Jannah* becomes necessary for him.'

I said: 'What a beautiful thing this is!' Then someone who was there before me said: 'The first was better than even this.' When I looked at him, I saw that it was ʿUmar (﷠) who said: 'I see that you have just come' and observed:

مَا مِنْكُمْ مِنْ أَحَدٍ يَتَوَضَّأُ فَيُبْلِغُ - أَوْ فَيُسْبِغُ - الْوُضُوءَ ثُمَّ يَقُولُ أَشْهَدُ أَنْ لاَ إِلَهَ إِلاَّ اللَّهُ وَأَنَّ مُحَمَّدًا عَبْدُ اللَّهِ وَرَسُولُهُ إِلاَّ فُتِحَتْ لَهُ أَبْوَابُ الْجَنَّةِ الثَّمَانِيَةُ يَدْخُلُ مِنْ أَيِّهَا شَاءَ

'If anyone amongst you performs the ablution, and then completes the ablution well and then says: 'I testify that there is no one worthy of worship except Allah and that Muhammad is the servant of Allah and His Messenger', the Eight Gates of *Jannah* would be opened for him and he may enter by whichever of them he wishes.' " (*Ṣaḥīḥ Muslim* 234 and *Sunan Abū Dāwūd* 169)

Jābir ibn ʿAbdillāh (﷠) reported: The Messenger of Allah (ﷺ) said:

مِفْتَاحُ الْجَنَّةِ الصَّلَاةُ وَمِفْتَاحُ الصَّلَاةِ الْوُضُوءُ

"The key to *Jannah* is prayer, and the key to prayer is ablution." (*Sunan al-Tirmidhī* 4)

4. *Before Ẓuhr prayer*

ʿAbdullāh ibn al-Sāʾib (ﷺ) reported:

"The Messenger of Allah (ﷺ) would pray four cycles after the decline of the sun before noon prayer and he would say:

إِنَّهَا سَاعَةٌ تُفْتَحُ فِيهَا أَبْوَابُ السَّمَاءِ وَأُحِبُّ أَنْ يَصْعَدَ لِي فِيهَا عَمَلٌ صَالِحٌ

'Verily, there is an hour in which the Gates of Heaven are opened and I love that my good deeds ascend during it.' " (*Sunan al-Tirmidhī* 478, *Ṣaḥīḥ*)

Abū Ayyūb (ﷺ) reported:

"The Prophet (ﷺ) would pray four cycles before noon prayer. It was said to him, 'You are always performing this prayer.' The Prophet (ﷺ) said:

إِنَّ أَبْوَابَ السَّمَاءِ تُفْتَحُ إِذَا زَالَتِ الشَّمْسُ فَلَا تُرْتَجُ حَتَّى يُصَلَّى الظُّهْرُ فَأُحِبُّ أَنْ يَصْعَدَ لِي إِلَى السَّمَاءِ خَيْرٌ

'Verily, the Gates of Heaven are opened when the sun begins to decline. They do not begin to close until the noon prayer is completed. Thus, I love for my good deeds to ascend to the heavens.' " (*Musnad Aḥmad* 23565, *Ṣaḥīḥ li-ghayrihī* (authentic due to external evidences), according to al-Arnāʾūṭ)

5. *Every morning*

Abū Hurayrah (ﷺ) reported: The Messenger of Allah (ﷺ) said:

إِنَّ مَلَكًا بِبَابٍ مِنْ أَبْوَابِ الْجَنَّةِ يَقُولُ مَنْ يُقْرِضِ الْيَوْمَ يُجْزَ غَدًا وَمَلَكٌ بِبَابٍ آخَرَ يَقُولُ اللَّهُمَّ أَعْطِ مُنْفِقًا خَلَفًا وَأَعْطِ مُمْسِكًا تَلَفًا

"Verily, there is an angel at a gate among the Gates of *Jannah*, saying: 'Whoever offers a good loan today will be rewarded tomorrow!' And there is an angel at another door, saying: 'O Allah, give repayment to one who spends in charity, and give destruction to one who withholds charity!' " (*Ṣaḥīḥ Ibn Ḥibbān* 3333, *Ṣaḥīḥ* according to al-Albānī)

6. *When a believer dies*

Al-Barāʾ ibn ʿĀzib (رضي الله عنه) reported: The Prophet (ﷺ) said:

إِنَّ الْعَبْدَ الْمُؤْمِنَ إِذَا كَانَ فِي انْقِطَاعٍ مِنَ الدُّنْيَا وَإِقْبَالٍ مِنَ الْآخِرَةِ نَزَلَ إِلَيْهِ مَلَائِكَةٌ مِنَ السَّمَاءِ بِيضُ الْوُجُوهِ كَأَنَّ وُجُوهَهُمُ الشَّمْسُ مَعَهُمْ كَفَنٌ مِنْ أَكْفَانِ الْجَنَّةِ وَحَنُوطٌ مِنْ حَنُوطِ الْجَنَّةِ حَتَّى يَجْلِسُوا مِنْهُ مَدَّ الْبَصَرِ ثُمَّ يَجِيءُ مَلَكُ الْمَوْتِ عَلَيْهِ السَّلَامُ حَتَّى يَجْلِسَ عِنْدَ رَأْسِهِ فَيَقُولُ أَيَّتُهَا النَّفْسُ الطَّيِّبَةُ اخْرُجِي إِلَى مَغْفِرَةٍ مِنَ اللهِ وَرِضْوَانٍ فَتَخْرُجُ تَسِيلُ كَمَا تَسِيلُ الْقَطْرَةُ مِنْ فِي السِّقَاءِ فَيَأْخُذُهَا فَإِذَا أَخَذَهَا لَمْ يَدَعُوهَا فِي يَدِهِ طَرْفَةَ عَيْنٍ حَتَّى يَأْخُذُوهَا فَيَجْعَلُوهَا فِي ذَلِكَ الْكَفَنِ وَفِي ذَلِكَ الْحَنُوطِ وَيَخْرُجُ مِنْهَا كَأَطْيَبِ نَفْحَةِ مِسْكٍ وُجِدَتْ عَلَى وَجْهِ الْأَرْضِ فَيَصْعَدُونَ بِهَا فَلَا يَمُرُّونَ يَعْنِي بِهَا عَلَى مَلَإٍ مِنَ الْمَلَائِكَةِ إِلَّا قَالُوا مَا هَذَا الرُّوحُ الطَّيِّبُ فَيَقُولُونَ فُلَانُ بْنُ فُلَانٍ بِأَحْسَنِ أَسْمَائِهِ الَّتِي كَانُوا يُسَمُّونَهُ بِهَا فِي الدُّنْيَا حَتَّى يَنْتَهُوا بِهَا إِلَى السَّمَاءِ الدُّنْيَا فَيَسْتَفْتِحُونَ لَهُ فَيُفْتَحُ لَهُمْ فَيُشَيِّعُهُ مِنْ كُلِّ سَمَاءٍ مُقَرَّبُوهَا إِلَى السَّمَاءِ الَّتِي تَلِيهَا حَتَّى يُنْتَهَى بِهِ إِلَى السَّمَاءِ السَّابِعَةِ فَيَقُولُ اللهُ عَزَّ وَجَلَّ اكْتُبُوا كِتَابَ عَبْدِي فِي عِلِّيِّينَ وَأَعِيدُوهُ إِلَى الْأَرْضِ فَإِنِّي مِنْهَا خَلَقْتُهُمْ وَفِيهَا أُعِيدُهُمْ وَمِنْهَا أُخْرِجُهُمْ تَارَةً أُخْرَى قَالَ فَتُعَادُ رُوحُهُ فِي جَسَدِهِ فَيَأْتِيهِ مَلَكَانِ فَيُجْلِسَانِهِ فَيَقُولَانِ لَهُ مَنْ رَبُّكَ فَيَقُولُ رَبِّيَ اللهُ فَيَقُولَانِ لَهُ مَا دِينُكَ فَيَقُولُ دِينِيَ الْإِسْلَامُ فَيَقُولَانِ لَهُ مَا هَذَا الرَّجُلُ الَّذِي بُعِثَ فِيكُمْ فَيَقُولُ هُوَ رَسُولُ اللهِ صَلَّى اللهُ عَلَيْهِ وَسَلَّمَ فَيَقُولَانِ لَهُ وَمَا عِلْمُكَ فَيَقُولُ قَرَأْتُ كِتَابَ اللهِ فَآمَنْتُ بِهِ وَصَدَّقْتُ فَيُنَادِي مُنَادٍ فِي السَّمَاءِ أَنْ صَدَقَ عَبْدِي فَأَفْرِشُوهُ مِنَ الْجَنَّةِ وَأَلْبِسُوهُ مِنَ الْجَنَّةِ وَافْتَحُوا لَهُ بَابًا إِلَى الْجَنَّةِ فَيَأْتِيهِ مِنْ رَوْحِهَا وَطِيبِهَا وَيُفْسَحُ لَهُ فِي قَبْرِهِ مَدَّ بَصَرِهِ وَيَأْتِيهِ رَجُلٌ

حَسَنُ الْوَجْهِ حَسَنُ الثِّيَابِ طَيِّبُ الرِّيحِ فَيَقُولُ أَبْشِرْ بِالَّذِي يَسُرُّكَ هَذَا يَوْمُكَ الَّذِي كُنْتَ تُوعَدُ فَيَقُولُ لَهُ مَنْ أَنْتَ فَوَجْهُكَ الْوَجْهُ يَجِيءُ بِالْخَيْرِ فَيَقُولُ أَنَا عَمَلُكَ

"Verily, when the believer is ready to depart the world and is facing the Hereafter, angels from heaven descend with bright faces, as if their faces were the sun, with them are the shrouds and perfumes of *Jannah*, until they sit from him a distance as far as the eye can see. Then, the angel of death, upon him be peace, comes until he sits by his head and he says: 'O pure soul, come out to the forgiveness of Allah and His pleasure!' He takes it out like a drop from a water-skin and holds it, never to leave his hand for the blink of an eye until he places it in that shroud and perfume. The scent coming from it is more pleasant than any musk you would find on the face of the earth. He ascends and passes by no gathering of angels but that they say: 'What a pure spirit!' They say he is this person, son of this person, calling him by the best names by which he was known in the world, until he stops at the lowest heaven and seeks entry and it will be opened for him. The company of each heaven bring him closer to the heaven following it until he stops at the seventh heaven. Allah the Almighty will say: 'Write the record of My servant in the righteous register and return him to the earth, for from it I created them, to it I return them, and from it I will take them out once again.' His spirit will be returned to his body and two angels will come to sit by him, saying to him: 'Who is your Lord?' He will say: 'My Lord is Allah.' They will say: 'What is your religion?' He will say: 'My religion is *Islām*.' They will say: 'Who is this man sent you?' He will say: 'He is the Messenger of Allah, peace and blessings be upon him.' They will say: 'How did you know?' He will say: 'I read the Book of Allah, had faith in it, and believed in it.' A heavenly announcement will be made: 'My servant has spoken the truth! Spread out carpets for him in *Jannah*, clothe him for *Jannah*, and open a gate for him to *Jannah*!' Its comforts and fragrances will come to him and his grave will become spacious as far as his eye can see. A handsome man, with fine clothes and a wonderful fragrance, will come and say: 'Glad tidings of what pleases you, for this was your day you were promised!' He will say: 'Who are you with such a handsome face?' He will say: 'I am your righteous deeds!' He will say: 'O Lord, begin the Hour that I may return to my family and property!' " (*Musnad Aḥmad* 18534, *Ṣaḥīḥ* according to al-Arnāʾūṭ)

When *Ramaḍān*'s blessed moon takes its ascent,
The gates of *Jannah* open, hearts repent.

On Mondays and Thursdays, a special grace,
Jannah's gates swing wide, in the reconciled's embrace.

After *wuḍū*'s cleansing, pure and clear,
Jannah's gates stand open, drawing near.

Before *Ẓuhr* prayer, as shadows gently sway,
The gates of Paradise invite us to obey.

With each new morning's light, a gift to cherish,
Jannah's gates unlock, our souls to nourish.

When a believer's journey on this earth is through,
Jannah's gates await, a welcome that is true.

In these moments, know Allah's mercy flows,
The gates of *Jannah* open, as faith steadily grows.

For Whom Will the Eight Gates of Jannah Be Opened?

1. *Whoever has the correct Tawḥīd*

ʿUbādah ibn al-Ṣāmit (ﷺ) reported: The Messenger of Allah (ﷺ) said:

مَنْ شَهِدَ أَنْ لاَ إِلَهَ إِلاَّ اللَّهُ وَحْدَهُ لاَ شَرِيكَ لَهُ وَأَنَّ مُحَمَّدًا عَبْدُهُ وَرَسُولُهُ وَأَنَّ عِيسَى عَبْدُ اللَّهِ وَرَسُولُهُ وَكَلِمَتُهُ أَلْقَاهَا إِلَى مَرْيَمَ وَرُوحٌ مِنْهُ وَالْجَنَّةُ حَقٌّ وَالنَّارُ حَقٌّ أَدْخَلَهُ اللَّهُ الْجَنَّةَ عَلَى مَا كَانَ مِنَ الْعَمَلِ

"Whoever testifies that there is no god but Allah alone without any partners, that Muhammad is His servant and His messenger, that Jesus is the servant of Allah and His messenger, His word which He bestowed upon Mary and a spirit from Him, and that *Jannah* is the truth and *Jahannam* is the truth, then Allah will admit him into *Jannah* by whatever good deeds he had done." (*Ṣaḥīḥ al-Bukhārī* 3435, *Ṣaḥīḥ Muslim* 28)

ʿUthmān (ﷺ) reported: The Messenger of Allah (ﷺ) said:

مَنْ مَاتَ وَهُوَ يَعْلَمُ أَنَّهُ لاَ إِلَهَ إِلاَّ اللَّهُ دَخَلَ الْجَنَّةَ

"He who died knowing that there is no one worthy of worship but Allah will enter *Jannah*." (*Ṣaḥīḥ Muslim* 26)

It was said to Wahb: "Is not the key to *Jannah* the declaration that there is no god but Allah?" Wahb said:

بَلَى وَلَكِنْ لَيْسَ مِفْتَاحٌ إِلَّا لَهُ أَسْنَانٌ فَإِنْ جِئْتَ بِمِفْتَاحٍ لَهُ أَسْنَانٌ فُتِحَ لَكَ وَإِلَّا لَمْ يُفْتَحْ لَكَ

"Of course, but rather every key has ridges. If you come with the correct key, the door will be opened for you. Otherwise, it will never be opened." (*Ṣaḥīḥ al-Bukhārī* 1180)

2. *Whoever has three (or two) children die before reaching puberty*

Muʿāwiyah ibn Qurrah (ﷺ) narrated that his father said:

"When the Prophet of Allah (ﷺ) sat, some of his Companions would sit with him. Among them was a man who had a little son who used to come to him from behind, and he would make him sit in front of him. He (the child) died, and the man stopped attending the circle because it reminded him of his son, and made him feel sad. The Prophet (ﷺ) missed him and said: 'Why do I not see so-and-so?' They said: 'O Messenger of Allah, his son whom you saw has died.' The Prophet (ﷺ) met him and asked him about his son, and he told him that he had died. He offered his condolences and said: 'O so-and-so, which would you like better, to enjoy his company all your life, or to come to any of the gates of *Jannah* on the Day of Resurrection, and find that he arrived there before you, and he is opening the gate for you?' He said: 'O Prophet of Allah! For him to get to the gate of *Jannah* before me and open it for me is dearer to me.' He said: 'You will have that.' A man asked: 'O Messenger of Allah (ﷺ)! Is this specially for him or for all of us?' He (ﷺ) said: 'But it is for all of you.' " (*Sunan al-Nasāʾī* 2088, *Ṣaḥīḥ*)

Anas (ﷺ) reported: The Messenger of Allah (ﷺ) said:

مَا مِنْ مُسلِمٍ يَمُوتُ لَهُ ثلاثَةٌ لَمْ يَبْلُغُوا الحِنْثَ إِلَّا أدخلَهُ اللَّهُ الجنَّةَ بِفَضْلِ رَحْمَتِهِ إِيَّاهُمْ

"Any *muslim* who loses (to death) three children before reaching puberty will be admitted by Allah into *Jannah* because of his being merciful to them." (*Ṣaḥīḥ al-Bukhārī* & *Ṣaḥīḥ Muslim*)

Muʿādh ibn Jabal (ﷺ) reported: The Prophet (ﷺ) said:

وَالَّذِي نَفْسِي بِيَدِهِ إِنَّ السِّقْطَ لَيَجُرُّ أُمَّهُ بِسَرَرِهِ إِلَى الْجَنَّةِ إِذَا احْتَسَبَتْهُ

"By the One in whose hand is my soul, the miscarried fetus will carry his mother by his umbilical cord into *Jannah*, if she was seeking its reward." (*Sunan Ibn Mājah* 1609, *Ṣaḥīḥ*)

Shuraḥbīl ibn Shufʿah (ﷺ) reported: The Prophet (ﷺ) said:

يُقَالُ لِلْوِلْدَانِ يَوْمَ الْقِيَامَةِ ادْخُلُوا الْجَنَّةَ قَالَ فَيَقُولُونَ يَا رَبِّ حَتَّى يَدْخُلَ آبَاؤُنَا وَأُمَّهَاتُنَا قَالَ فَيَأْتُونَ قَالَ فَيَقُولُ اللَّهُ عَزَّ وَجَلَّ مَا لِي أَرَاهُمْ مُحْبَنْطِئِينَ ادْخُلُوا الْجَنَّةَ قَالَ فَيَقُولُونَ يَا رَبِّ آبَاؤُنَا وَأُمَّهَاتُنَا قَالَ فَيَقُولُ ادْخُلُوا الْجَنَّةَ أَنْتُمْ وَآبَاؤُكُمْ

"It will be said to children on the Day of Resurrection: 'Enter *Jannah*.' They will say: 'Our Lord, not unless our fathers and mothers enter.' Allah the Almighty will say: 'Why do I see them hesitant to enter *Jannah*?' They will say: 'O Lord, our fathers and mothers.' Allah will say: 'Enter *Jannah*, all of you and your parents.' " (*Musnad Aḥmad* 16971, *Jayyid* (good) according to al-Arnāʾūṭ)

Jābir ibn ʿAbdillāh (ﷺ) reported: The Messenger of Allah (ﷺ) said:

مَنْ كُنَّ لَهُ ثَلَاثُ بَنَاتٍ يُؤْوِيهِنَّ وَيَرْحَمُهُنَّ وَيَكْفُلُهُنَّ وَجَبَتْ لَهُ الْجَنَّةُ الْبَتَّةَ قَالَ قِيلَ يَا رَسُولَ اللَّهِ فَإِنْ كَانَتْ اثْنَتَيْنِ قَالَ وَإِنْ كَانَتْ اثْنَتَيْنِ قَالَ فَرَأَى بَعْضُ الْقَوْمِ أَنْ لَوْ قَالُوا لَهُ وَاحِدَةً لَقَالَ وَاحِدَةً

" 'Whoever has three daughters and he cares for them, he is merciful to them, and he clothes them, then *Jannah* is *Wājib* upon him.' It was said, 'O Messenger of Allah, what if he has only two?' The Prophet (ﷺ) said, 'Even two.' Some people thought that if they had said to him one, the Prophet (ﷺ) would have said even one." (*Musnad Aḥmad* 14247, *Ṣaḥīḥ* according to al-Arnāʾūṭ)

Abū Saʿīd al-Khudrī (ﷺ) reported: The Messenger of Allah (ﷺ) said:

لَا يَكُونُ لِأَحَدٍ ثَلَاثُ بَنَاتٍ أَوْ ثَلَاثُ أَخَوَاتٍ أَوْ ابْنَتَانِ أَوْ أُخْتَانِ فَيَتَّقِي اللَّهَ فِيهِنَّ وَيُحْسِنُ إِلَيْهِنَّ إِلَّا دَخَلَ الْجَنَّةَ

"There is not one of you with three daughters or three sisters, or two daughters or two sisters, fearing Allah regarding them and treating them in the best manner, but that he will enter *Jannah*." (*Musnad Aḥmad* 11384, *Ṣaḥīḥ li-ghayrihī* (authentic due to external evidences), according to al-Arnāʾūṭ)

3. *Whoever prays the five daily prayers and abstains from major sins.*

ʿAbdullāh ibn ʿAmr (ﷺ) reported: The Prophet (ﷺ) ascended the pulpit and said:

لَا أُقْسِمُ، لَا أُقْسِمُ، لَا أُقْسِمُ

"I take an oath (by Allah)! I take an oath (by Allah)! I take an oath (by Allah)!" He (ﷺ) then descended therefrom and said:

أَبْشِرُوا أَبْشِرُوا، إنه مَنْ صَلَّى الصَّلَوَاتِ الْخَمْسَ وَاجْتَنَبَ الْكَبَائِرَ دَخَلَ مِنْ أَبْوَابِ الْجَنَّةِ شَاءَ

"Rejoice! Rejoice! Verily, whoever performs the five prayers and avoids the major sins will enter Jannah from whichever gate he wishes." (*al-Muʿjam al-Kabīr lil-Ṭabarānī* 13/8, *Ḥasan* according to al-Albānī)

4. *An obedient and dutiful wife*

Abū Hurayrah (رضي الله عنه) reported: The Prophet (ﷺ) said:

إِذَا صَلَّتْ الْمَرْأَةُ خَمْسَهَا وَصَامَتْ شَهْرَهَا وَحَفِظَتْ فَرْجَهَا وَأَطَاعَتْ زَوْجَهَا قِيلَ لَهَا ادْخُلِي الْجَنَّةَ مِنْ أَيِّ أَبْوَابِ الْجَنَّةِ شِئْتِ

"If a woman prays her five (daily prayers), fasts her month (*Ramaḍān*), guards her chastity and obeys her husband, it will be said to her: 'Enter *Jannah* by whichever of the Gates of *Jannah* you wish.' " (*Musnad Aḥmad* 1664, *Ḥasan*, *Ṣaḥīḥ Ibn Ḥibbān* 4252, *Ṣaḥīḥ* according to al-Arnāʾūṭ)

5. *A shahīd (martyr)*

ʿUtbah ibn ʿAbd al-Sulamī (رضي الله عنه) narrates: The Messenger of Allah (ﷺ) said:

الْقَتْلى ثَلاثَةٌ : رَجُلٌ مُؤْمِنٌ قَاتَلَ بِنَفْسِهِ وَمَالِهِ فِي سَبِيلِ اللَّهِ حَتَّى إِذَا لَقِيَ الْعَدُوَّ قَاتَلَهُمْ حَتَّى يُقْتَلَ , فَذَلِكَ الشَّهِيدُ الْمُمْتَحَنُ فِي خَيْمَةِ اللَّهِ تَحْتَ عَرْشِهِ , لا يَفْضُلُهُ النَّبِيُّونَ إِلا بِدَرَجَةِ النُّبُوَّةِ ، وَرَجُلٌ مُؤْمِنٌ قَرَفَ عَلَى نَفْسِهِ مِنْ الذُّنُوبِ وَالْخَطَايَا جَاهَدَ بِنَفْسِهِ وَمَالِهِ فِي سَبِيلِ اللَّهِ حَتَّى إِذَا لَقِيَ الْعَدُوَّ قَاتَلَ حَتَّى يُقْتَلَ، مُحِيَتْ ذُنُوبُهُ وَخَطَايَاهُ , إِنَّ السَّيْفَ مَحَّاءُ الْخَطَايَا, وَأُدْخِلَ مِنْ أَيِّ أَبْوَابِ الْجَنَّةِ شَاءَ , فَإِنَّ لَهَا ثَمَانِيَةَ أَبْوَابٍ , وَلِجَهَنَّمَ سَبْعَةَ أَبْوَابٍ , وَبَعْضُهَا أَفْضَلُ مِنْ بَعْضٍ ، وَرَجُلٌ مُنَافِقٌ جَاهَدَ بِنَفْسِهِ وَمَالِهِ حَتَّى إِذَا لَقِيَ الْعَدُوَّ قَاتَلَ فِي سَبِيلِ اللَّهِ حَتَّى يُقْتَلَ فَإِنَّ ذَلِكَ فِي النَّارِ , السَّيْفُ لا يَمْحُو النِّفَاقَ

"A *mujāhid* can be of three types. A believer who fights in the way of Allah with his life and wealth, and when he encounters an enemy, he fights until he is killed. He is the purified (tested/patient) martyr who will be in the tent under the Throne of Allah. The difference, in rank, between he and the prophets is due to their prophethood.

The second is the believer who has committed sins, then fights in the way of Allah with his life and wealth until he is killed. He will be cleansed from sins, as wielding a sword in the way of Allah removes sins. He will be allowed to enter through any of the Gates of *Jannah*. *Jannah* has eight gates, and *Jahannam* has seven gates, and some of them are lower than others.

The third is a hypocrite who fights in the path of Allah with his life and wealth and gets killed. But he will go to *Jahannam* as the sword does not clean hypocrisy." (*Musnad Aḥmad* 17204, *Ḥasan* according to al-Albānī in *Ṣaḥīḥ al-Targhīb* 1370)

For those with *tawḥīd*, gates of *Jannah* wide,
Their faith unwavering, in Allah's light they bide.

Three children's innocence, before adulthood's dawn,
The gates swing open, in Paradise they're drawn.

Five daily prayers, from major sins abstain,
Jannah's gates for them, a heavenly domain.

An obedient wife, her virtue shining bright,
The gates of *Jannah* gleam with pure delight.

A *shahīd*'s sacrifice, in battles fierce and wild,
The gates of Paradise, all for them compiled.

In these noble souls, Allah's grace is seen,
For whom the gates of *Jannah* shine, serene.

Distance Between the Gates of Jannah

1. *The distance between Makkah and Buṣrā*

Abū Hurayrah (ﷺ) reported (in a lengthy *ḥadīth*): The Prophet (ﷺ) said:

وَالَّذِي نَفْسِي بِيَدِهِ إِنَّ مَا بَيْنَ الْمِصْرَاعَيْنِ مِنْ مَصَارِيعِ الْجَنَّةِ كَمَا بَيْنَ مَكَّةَ وَحِمْيَرَ، أَوْ كَمَا بَيْنَ مَكَّةَ وَبُصْرَى

"By the One in whose hand is the soul of Muhammad, the distance between two panels of the Gates of *Jannah* or between the two gateposts, is like the distance between *Makkah* and *Ḥimyar* (Yemen), or between *Makkah* and *Buṣrā* (city in Syria/Damascus). (*Ṣaḥīḥ al-Bukhārī* 4712, and *Ṣaḥīḥ Muslim* 194)

Muslim's wording states the city as *Hajar* (Bahrain) instead of *Ḥimyar*.

2. *The distance of forty years*

Abū Saʿīd al-Khudrī (ﷺ) and Muʿāwiyah ibn Ḥaydah (ﷺ) narrated: The Prophet (ﷺ) said:

مَا بَيْنَ مِصْرَاعَيْنِ فِي الْجَنَّةِ كَمَسِيرَةِ أَرْبَعِينَ سَنَةً

"The distance between the two gate-panels of one of the gates of *Jannah* is the distance of forty years, but a time will come when it would be very crowded." (*Musnad Aḥmad*, *Ṣaḥīḥ* according to al-Albānī)

There is a similar *ḥadīth* from ʿUtbah ibn Ghazwān (ﷺ) stating:

"It has been mentioned that there yawns a distance which one would be able to cover in forty years from one end to another of *Jannah*, and a day would come when it would be fully packed." (*Ṣaḥīḥ Muslim* 2967, *Mursal*)

ʿAbdullāh ibn Salām (ﷺ) narrated: The Prophet (ﷺ) said:

إِنَّ مَا بَيْنَ مِصْرَاعَيِ الجَنَّةِ مِقْدَارُ أَرْبَعِينَ عَامًا، وَلَيَأْتِيَنَّ عَلَيْهِ يَوْمًا يُزَاحَمُ عَلَيْهِ كَازْدِحَامِ الإِبِلِ وَرَدَتْ لِخَمْسٍ ظِمَاءً

"The distance between the two gate-panels of *Jannah* is the distance of forty years. And a time will come when it (the gate) will become as crowded as a drinking-trough surrounded by thirsty camels." (*al-Ṭabarānī al-Muʿjam al-Kabīr* 14970, *Ṣaḥīḥ* according to al-Albānī)

Ibn al-Qayyim (ﷺ) stated:

"The *ḥadith* of forty years distance may be referring to one of the greatest doors of *Jannah*." (*Ḥādī al-Arwāḥ*, 115)

Al-Ṣanʿanī (ﷺ) stated:

"The gates of *Jannah* vary in their distance. Some are the distance between *Makkah* and *Hajar* and others are forty years in distance." (*al-Tanwīr Sharḥ al-Jāmiʿ al-Ṣaghīr*, vol. 4, 522-523)

In *Jannah*'s gates, a vast expanse is seen,
As told by the Prophet, in words pristine.

The distance spans like Makkah's sacred ground,
To distant lands where heavenly grace is found.

Between two panels, gateposts wide apart,
A journey waits, where blissful dreams may start.

For forty years, they stand as a divide,
Yet in a crowded future, they'll coincide.

A scene where hearts of faithful souls will throng,
As camels gather 'round a watering song.

These gates, they vary in their vast expanse,
Some wider than the eye can hope to glance.

In Paradise's embrace, they welcome all,
Each gate, a wondrous tale for hearts to call.

So strive, O souls, toward *Jannah*'s radiant gleam,
Where gates are vast, and love's the eternal theme.

GATES OF JANNAH

There are 8 gates of *Jannah*, 4 of which have been mentioned in one *ḥadīth* and 4 on which the scholars have differed. I will mention all the different gates according to the various opinions of the scholars.

Abū Hurayrah (ﷺ) narrates that the Prophet (ﷺ) said:

مَنْ أَنْفَقَ زَوْجَيْنِ فِي سَبِيلِ اللَّهِ نُودِيَ مِنْ أَبْوَابِ الْجَنَّةِ يَا عَبْدَ اللَّهِ هَذَا خَيْرٌ فَمَنْ كَانَ مِنْ أَهْلِ الصَّلَاةِ دُعِيَ مِنْ بَابِ الصَّلَاةِ وَمَنْ كَانَ مِنْ أَهْلِ الْجِهَادِ دُعِيَ مِنْ بَابِ الْجِهَادِ وَمَنْ كَانَ مِنْ أَهْلِ الصِّيَامِ دُعِيَ مِنْ بَابِ الرَّيَّانِ وَمَنْ كَانَ مِنْ أَهْلِ الصَّدَقَةِ دُعِيَ مِنْ بَابِ الصَّدَقَةِ فَقَالَ أَبُو بَكْرٍ رَضِيَ اللَّهُ عَنْهُ بِأَبِي أَنْتَ وَأُمِّي يَا رَسُولَ اللَّهِ مَا عَلَى مَنْ دُعِيَ مِنْ تِلْكَ الْأَبْوَابِ مِنْ ضَرُورَةٍ فَهَلْ يُدْعَى أَحَدٌ مِنْ تِلْكَ الْأَبْوَابِ كُلِّهَا قَالَ نَعَمْ وَأَرْجُو أَنْ تَكُونَ مِنْهُمْ

" 'Anyone who spends a pair (2 dinārs, 2 dirhams or any 2 things or is habitual in spending) in the way of Allah will be called from all the gates of *Jannah*: 'O servant of Allah, this is good!' The people of prayer will be called from the Gate of Prayer, the people of jihad will be called from the Gate of Jihad, the people of fasting will be called from the Gate of *al-Rayyān*, and the people of charity will be called from the Gate of Charity.' Abū Bakr (ﷺ) said, 'One who is called from all those gates would need nothing. Will anyone be called from all those gates, O Messenger of Allah?' The Prophet (ﷺ) said, 'Yes, and I hope you will be among them, O Abū Bakr.' " (*Ṣaḥīḥ al-Bukhārī* 3666, *Ṣaḥīḥ Muslim* 1027)

The Gates of *Jannah*, narrations do proclaim,
Are distant, yet each has a unique name.

A journey between them, vast and wide,
With deeds and faith, we'll cross that divide.

The fasting's gate is **al-Rayyān**, we're told,
For those most patient, their hearts made of gold.

Then **Bāb al-Ṣalāh**, where prayers ascend,
Worshipful and diligent, their hearts forever mend.

Al-Ṣadaqah's gate, the generous shall find,
The distance measured by the generous heart's bind.

Al-Jihād's entrance, for those who strive,
The distance here, with valour, they'll arrive.

Al-Kāẓimīn al-Ghayẓ, a gate of gentle grace,
Forgiving and merciful, they'll surely find their place.

For pilgrims of Hajj, **Bāb al-Ḥājj**, the door,
The distance traversed by those who implore.

Bāb al-Dhikr, where remembrance resides,
The distance covered by mindful strides.

Bāb al-Wālid, a righteous child's abode,
With dutiful hearts, along this path we're towed.

To these gates be our calling, our faith's our guide,
Through *Jannah*'s gates, we'll eventually reside.

CHAPTER

One

BĀB UMMAT MUḤAMMAD (ﷺ)

A SPECIAL GATE FOR THE UMMAH OF THE PROPHET (ﷺ)

1. *Bāb Ummat-Muḥammad (ﷺ) – A Special Gate for the Ummah of the Prophet (ﷺ)*

Sālim ibn ʿAbdillāh (ﷺ) narrated from his father that the Messenger of Allah (ﷺ) said:

بَابُ أُمَّتِي الَّذِي يَدْخُلُونَ مِنْهُ الجَنَّةَ عَرْضُهُ مَسِيرَةُ الرَّاكِبِ الْمُجَوِّدِ ثَلاثًا، ثُمَّ إِنَّهُمْ لَيُضْغَطُونَ عَلَيْهِ حَتَّى تَكَادَ مَنَاكِبُهُمْ تَزُولُ

"The distance of the gate through which my *Ummah* will enter *Jannah* is the distance that a good rider covers in three (meaning three nights or three years, and the latter is more apparent). Despite that, they shall be constrained by it until their shoulders are almost crushed completely. (*Sunan al-Tirmidhī*, 2548, Weak)

Abū Hurayrah (ﷺ) narrated: The Prophet (ﷺ) said:

أَتَانِي جِبْرِيلُ فَأَخَذَ بِيَدِي فَأَرَانِي بَابَ الْجَنَّةِ الَّذِي تَدْخُلُ مِنْهُ أُمَّتِي. فَقَالَ أَبُو بَكْرٍ يَا رَسُولَ اللَّهِ وَدِدْتُ أَنِّي كُنْتُ مَعَكَ حَتَّى أَنْظُرَ إِلَيْهِ . فَقَالَ رَسُولُ اللَّهِ صلى الله عليه وسلم: أَمَا إِنَّكَ يَا أَبَا بَكْرٍ أَوَّلُ مَنْ يَدْخُلُ الْجَنَّةَ مِنْ أُمَّتِي

"Jibrīl (ﷺ) came and took me by the hand and showed the gate of *Jannah* by which my *Ummah* will enter." Abū Bakr (ﷺ) then said: "O Messenger of Allah! I wish I had been with you so that I might have looked at it." The Messenger of Allah (ﷺ) then said: "You, Abū Bakr, will be the first of my *Ummah* to enter *Jannah*." (*Sunan Abū Dāwūd* 4652, Weak)

Ibn al-Qayyim (ﷺ) stated:

وَلِهذِهِ الأُمَّةِ بَابٌ مُختَصٌّ بِهِم يَدْخُلُونَ مِنه دُونَ سَائِرِ الأُمَم.

"For this *Ummah*, there is a special gate that is assigned for them to enter *Jannah* through it exclusively." (*Ḥādī al-Arwāḥ*)

Bāb Ummat-Muḥammad, a gate divine and rare,
For the Prophet's followers, it's a treasure to declare.

The distance to this gateway, a rider's three-year ride,
Through it they will rush, entering side by side.

Constrained by its embrace, their shoulders almost crushed,
Yet they'll strive to enter, in Allah's mercy, they're hushed.

Jibrīl did once revealed it before the Prophet's sight,
A gate of the Gates of *Jannah*, where believers find delight.

Abū Bakr yearned to witness its beauty and its grace,
But the Prophet's promise, his heart would soon embrace.

For Abū Bakr, the first, in *Jannah*'s realms he'd soar,
Through Bāb Ummat-Muḥammad, to Paradise's open door.

CHAPTER

Two

BĀB AL-ṢALĀH

GATE OF PRAYER

a. *Duʿā after wuḍūʾ will open all the Gates of Jannah*

ʿUqbah ibn ʿĀmir (🙏) reported:

We were entrusted with the task of tending the camels. On my turn when I came back in the evening after grazing them in the pastures, I found Allah's Messenger (🙏) standing and addressing the people. I heard these words of his:

مَا مِنْ مُسْلِمٍ يَتَوَضَّأُ فَيُحْسِنُ وُضُوءَهُ ثُمَّ يَقُومُ فَيُصَلِّي رَكْعَتَيْنِ مُقْبِلٌ عَلَيْهِمَا بِقَلْبِهِ وَوَجْهِهِ إِلاَّ وَجَبَتْ لَهُ الْجَنَّةُ

"There is no *muslim* who performs ablution properly, then gets up and offers two *rakaʿāt* turning to them wholeheartedly, except that *Jannah* becomes necessary for him."

I said: What a beautiful thing this is! Then someone who was there before me said: The first was better than even this. When I looked at him, I saw that it was ʿUmar (🙏) who said: I see that you have just come and observed:

مَا مِنْكُمْ مِنْ أَحَدٍ يَتَوَضَّأُ فَيُبْلِغُ - أَوْ فَيُسْبِغُ - الْوُضُوءَ ثُمَّ يَقُولُ أَشْهَدُ أَنْ لاَ إِلَهَ إِلاَّ اللَّهُ وَأَنَّ مُحَمَّدًا عَبْدُ اللَّهِ وَرَسُولُهُ إِلاَّ فُتِحَتْ لَهُ أَبْوَابُ الْجَنَّةِ الثَّمَانِيَةُ يَدْخُلُ مِنْ أَيِّهَا شَاءَ

"If anyone amongst you performs the ablution, and then completes the ablution well and then says: I testify that there is no one worthy of worship except Allah and that Muhammad is the servant of Allah and His Messenger, the Eight Gates of *Jannah* would be opened for him and he may enter by whichever of them he wishes." (*Ṣaḥīḥ Muslim* 234 and *Sunan Abū Dāwūd* 169)

b. Key to Jannah

Jābir ibn ʿAbdillāh (ﷺ) reported: The Messenger of Allah (ﷺ) said:

مِفْتَاحُ الْجَنَّةِ الصَّلَاةُ وَمِفْتَاحُ الصَّلَاةِ الْوُضُوءُ

"The key to *Jannah* is prayer, and the key to prayer is ablution." (*Sunan al-Tirmidhī* 4)

c. Taḥiyyat al-Wuḍūʾ

ʿUqbah ibn ʿĀmir (ﷺ) reported: The Messenger of Allah (ﷺ) said:

مَا مِنْ مُسْلِمٍ يَتَوَضَّأُ فَيُحْسِنُ وُضُوءَهُ ثُمَّ يَقُومُ فَيُصَلِّي رَكْعَتَيْنِ مُقْبِلٌ عَلَيْهِمَا بِقَلْبِهِ وَوَجْهِهِ إِلَّا وَجَبَتْ لَهُ الْجَنَّةُ

"No *muslim* performs ablution well and then prays two cycles with his heart and direction focused, except that *Jannah* will be necessary for him." (*Ṣaḥīḥ Muslim* 234)

Abū Hurayrah (ﷺ) reported: The Prophet (ﷺ) said to Bilāl (ﷺ) at the time of *Fajr* prayer:

يَا بِلَالُ حَدِّثْنِي بِأَرْجَى عَمَلٍ عَمِلْتَهُ فِي الْإِسْلَامِ فَإِنِّي سَمِعْتُ دَفَّ نَعْلَيْكَ بَيْنَ يَدَيَّ فِي الْجَنَّةِ قَالَ مَا عَمِلْتُ عَمَلًا أَرْجَى عِنْدِي أَنِّي لَمْ أَتَطَهَّرْ طَهُورًا فِي سَاعَةِ لَيْلٍ أَوْ نَهَارٍ إِلَّا صَلَّيْتُ بِذَلِكَ الطُّهُورِ مَا كُتِبَ لِي أَنْ أُصَلِّيَ

"O Bilāl, tell me of the most hopeful deed you practiced in *Islām*. I heard the scuffle of your sandals before me in *Jannah*." Bilāl said, "The most hopeful deed to me is that I do not perform ablution by day or night but that I pray along with it as much as Allah has decreed me to pray." (*Ṣaḥīḥ al-Bukhārī* 1149, *Ṣaḥīḥ Muslim* 2458)

d. *Ṣalāt al-Ḍuḥā is rewarded with a castle*

Anas ibn Mālik (ﷺ) narrated: The Prophet (ﷺ)said:

من صلَّى الضُّحى ثنتي عشرةَ ركعةً بنى اللَّهُ لهُ قصرًا من ذهبٍ في الجنَّةِ

"Whoever prays the twelve *rakaʿāt* of *Ḍuḥā*, Allah will build for him a palace of gold in *Jannah*." (*Mishkāt al-Maṣābīḥ*, *Ḥasan* according to Ibn Ḥajar in *Takhrīj Mishkāt al-Maṣābīḥ* 2/74, and Ibn al-Mulaqqin in *Tuḥfat al-Muḥtāj* 1/415. Classified as *Gharīb* by al-Tirmidhī, and *Ḍaʿīf* by al-Albānī)

e. *Six rakaʿāt after Maghrib*

Abū Hurayrah (ﷺ) narrates: The Prophet (ﷺ) said:

مَنْ صَلَّى بَعْدَ الْمَغْرِبِ سِتَّ رَكَعَاتٍ لَمْ يَتَكَلَّمْ فِيمَا بَيْنَهُنَّ بِسُوءٍ عُدِلْنَ لَهُ بِعِبَادَةِ ثِنْتَيْ عَشْرَةَ سَنَةً

"Whoever prays, after *Maghrib*, six *rakaʿāt* without talking anything indecent in between them, it would be equivalent to twelve years of worship for him." (*Sunan al-Tirmidhī* 435, Very Weak, *Sunan Ibn Mājah* 1167, Weak)

However, it is proven that the Prophet (ﷺ) did pray between *Maghrib* and *ʿIshāʾ*.

Ḥudhayfah (ﷺ) narrates: I came to the Prophet (ﷺ) and prayed *Maghrib* with him. When he had finished the prayer, he stood and prayed, and he kept praying until he prayed *ʿIshāʾ*. (*Musnad Aḥmad* 22926, *Ṣaḥīḥ* according to al-Albānī, *Irwāʾ al-Ghalīl* 470)

It is also proven from some of the *Ṣaḥābah* that they used to pray between *Maghrib* and *ʿIshāʾ*. Anas ibn Mālik (ﷺ) said, concerning the verse:

تَتَجَافَىٰ جُنُوبُهُمْ عَنِ ٱلْمَضَاجِعِ يَدْعُونَ رَبَّهُمْ خَوْفًا وَطَمَعًا وَمِمَّا رَزَقْنَـٰهُمْ يُنفِقُونَ ﴿١٦﴾

"Their sides part (i.e., they arise) from [their] beds; they supplicate their Lord in fear and aspiration, and from what We have provided them, they spend." (*al-Sajdah*, 32:16)

They used to wake up and pray *Nafl* between *Maghrib* and *ʿIshāʾ*.

Al-Ḥasan (ﷺ) used to say: [This is referring to] *Qiyām al-Layl*. (Abū Dāwūd 1321, *Ṣaḥīḥ* according to al-Albānī in *Ṣaḥīḥ Abū Dāwūd*)

Ibn Mardawayh (ﷺ) narrated in his *Tafsīr* that Anas (ﷺ) said concerning this verse: They would pray between *Maghrib* and *ʿIshāʾ*. (Ḥāfiẓ al-ʿIrāqī said: Its chain is *Jayyid* (good), *ʿAwn al-Maʿbūd*)

f. ***Twelve rakaʿāt Nawāfil during the day will give you a house in Jannah***

Umm Ḥabībah (ﷺ) reported: The Messenger of Allah (ﷺ) said:

مَنْ صَلَّى اثْنَتَيْ عَشْرَةَ رَكْعَةً فِي يَوْمٍ وَلَيْلَةٍ بُنِيَ لَهُ بِهِنَّ بَيْتٌ فِي الْجَنَّةِ

"Whoever performs twelve cycles of prayer in each day and night, a house in *Jannah* will be built for them through this."

Umm Ḥabībah said: "I have never abandoned them since I heard it from the Messenger of Allah (ﷺ)." (*Ṣaḥīḥ Muslim* 728)

g. ***Āyat al-Kursī after prayer will make you enter Jannah***

Abū Umāmah (ﷺ) reported: The Messenger of Allah (ﷺ) said:

مَنْ قَرَأَ آيَةَ الْكُرْسِيِّ دُبُرَ كُلِّ صَلَاةٍ مَكْتُوبَةٍ لَمْ يَمْنَعْهُ مِنْ دُخُولِ الْجَنَّةِ إِلَّا أَنْ يَمُوت

"Whoever recites the 'Verse of the Throne' after every prescribed prayer, there will be nothing standing between him and entry into *Jannah* but his death." (*al-Muʿjam al-Awsaṭ lil-Ṭabarānī* 8068, *Ṣaḥīḥ* according to al-Albānī, *al-Nasāʾī* 100, *Ṣaḥīḥ* in *ʿAmal al-Yawm wa-l-Laylah*)

h. ***Repeating the words of the adhān will make you enter Jannah***

Ibn ʿUmar (ﷺ) narrated: The Messenger of Allah (ﷺ) said:

من أذَّنَ ثِنتَي عشرةَ سنةً ، وجبَتْ له الجنَّةُ ، وَكُتبَ لَه بتأذينِهِ في كلِّ يومٍ ستُّونَ حسَنةً ، ولِكُلِّ إقامةٍ ثلاثون حَسنةً

"Whoever gives the call to prayer for twelve years will be guaranteed *Jannah*, and for each day sixty rewards will be recorded for him by virtue of his *adhān*, and thirty rewards by virtue of his *iqāmah*." (*Sunan Ibn Mājah* 728; *Ṣaḥīḥ* according to al-Mundhirī and al-Albānī, *Ṣaḥīḥ al-Targhīb*, 248)

ʿUmar ibn al-Khaṭṭāb (ﷺ) narrated: The Prophet (ﷺ) said:

إذا قالَ المُؤَذِّنُ: اللَّهُ أكبَرُ اللَّهُ أكبَرُ، فقالَ أحَدُكُمْ: اللَّهُ أكْبَرُ اللَّهُ أكبَرُ، ثُمَّ قالَ: أشْهَدُ أنْ لا إلَهَ إلَّا اللَّهُ، قالَ: أشْهَدُ أنْ لا إلَهَ إلَّا اللَّهُ، ثُمَّ قالَ: أشْهَدُ أنَّ مُحَمَّدًا رَسولُ اللهِ قالَ: أشْهَدُ أنَّ مُحَمَّدًا رَسولُ اللهِ، ثُمَّ قالَ: حَيَّ علَى الصَّلاةِ، قالَ: لا حَوْلَ ولا قُوَّةَ إلَّا باللَّهِ، ثُمَّ قالَ: حَيَّ علَى الفَلاحِ، قالَ: لا حَوْلَ ولا قُوَّةَ إلَّا باللَّهِ، ثُمَّ قالَ: اللَّهُ أكْبَرُ اللَّهُ أكبَرُ، قالَ: اللَّهُ أكْبَرُ اللَّهُ أكبَرُ، ثُمَّ قالَ: لا إلَهَ إلَّا اللَّهُ، قالَ: لا إلَهَ إلَّا اللَّهُ مِن قَلْبِهِ دَخَلَ الجَنَّةَ

"When the caller to prayer says, 'Allah is the greatest, Allah is the greatest,' then let one of you say: 'Allah is the greatest, Allah is the greatest.' Then he says, 'I testify there is no god but Allah,' one says, 'I testify there is no god but Allah.' Then he says, 'I testify Muhammad is the Messenger of Allah,' one says, 'I testify Muhammad is the Messenger of Allah.' Then he says, 'Come to prayer,' one says, 'There is no power nor strength except through Allah.' Then he says, 'Come to salvation,' one says, 'There is no power nor strength except through Allah.' Then he says, 'Allah is the greatest, Allah is the greatest,' one says, 'Allah is the greatest, Allah is the greatest.' Then he says, 'There is no god but Allah,' one says, 'There is no god but Allah'—[whoever says all this] from his heart will enter *Jannah*." (*Ṣaḥīḥ Muslim* 385)

Abū Hurayrah (ﷺ) reported: We were with the Messenger of Allah (ﷺ) when Bilāl (ﷺ) stood to announce the prayer, then he was silent. The Prophet (ﷺ) said:

مَنْ قَالَ مِثْلَ هَذَا يَقِينًا دَخَلَ الْجَنَّةَ

"Whoever says the likes of this with conviction, he will enter *Jannah*." (*Sunan al-Nasāʾī* 674, *Ṣaḥīḥ* according to al-Albānī)

ʿAbdullāh ibn ʿAmr (ﷺ) reported: A man said: "O Messenger of Allah, the callers to prayer have been favored over us." The Messenger of Allah (ﷺ) said:

قُلْ كَمَا يَقُولُونَ فَإِذَا انْتَهَيْتَ فَسَلْ تُعْطَهْ

"Say as they have said. When you have finished, ask Allah and you will receive." (*Sunan Abī Dāwūd* 524, *Ṣaḥīḥ* according to Aḥmad Shākir)

Anas ibn Mālik (ﷺ) reported: The Messenger of Allah (ﷺ) said:

الدُّعَاءُ لَا يُرَدُّ بَيْنَ الْأَذَانِ وَالْإِقَامَةِ

"Supplication is not rejected between the call to prayer and its commencement."

They said: "What should we say, O Messenger of Allah?" The Prophet (ﷺ) said:

سَلُوا اللَّهَ الْعَافِيَةَ فِي الدُّنْيَا وَالْآخِرَةِ

"Ask Allah for wellness in the world and in the Hereafter." (*Sunan al-Tirmidhī* 3594, *Ṣaḥīḥ* according to Ibn al-Qayyim)

i. ***Four Sunnah of Ẓuhr will forbid Jahannam for you***

Umm Ḥabībah (رضي الله عنها) reported: The Messenger of Allah (ﷺ) said:

مَنْ حَافَظَ عَلَى أَرْبَعِ رَكَعَاتٍ قَبْلَ الظُّهْرِ وَأَرْبَعٍ بَعْدَهَا حَرَّمَهُ اللَّهُ عَلَى النَّارِ

"Whoever preserves four cycles of prayer before noon prayer and after it, Allah will forbid him from entering *Jahannam*." (*Sunan al-Tirmidhī* 428, *Ṣaḥīḥ*, *Sunan al-Nasāʾī* 1817)

j. ***Tahajjud prayer will help you to enter Jannah***

ʿAbdullāh ibn Salām (رضي الله عنه) narrates: The first thing I heard the Prophet (ﷺ) say when he arrived in *Madīnah*:

يَا أَيُّهَا النَّاسُ أَفْشُوا السَّلَامَ وَأَطْعِمُوا الطَّعَامَ وَصِلُوا الأَرْحَامَ وَصَلُّوا بِاللَّيْلِ وَالنَّاسُ نِيَامٌ تَدْخُلُوا الْجَنَّةَ بِسَلَامٍ

"O people, spread the *Salām*, feed the people, keep the ties of kinship, and pray during the night while others are asleep and you will enter *Jannah* in peace." (*Sunan Ibn Mājah* 3251, *Ṣaḥīḥ*, *Sunan al-Tirmidhī* 2485, *Ṣaḥīḥ*)

k. Freedom from hypocrisy and Jahannam

Anas ibn Mālik (ﷺ) narrated: The Prophet (ﷺ) said:

مَنْ صلَّى للهِ أربعينَ يومًا في جماعةٍ ، يُدْرِكُ التَّكْبيرَةَ الأُولَى ، كُتِبَتْ لهُ بَرَاءَتَانِ : بَرَاءَةٌ مِنَ النارِ، و بَرَاءَةٌ مِنَ النِّفَاقِ

"Whoever prays to Allah for forty days in congregation, catching up with the first *takbīr*, he will be recorded as being free from two things: free from *Jahannam*, and free from hypocrisy." (*Sunan al-Tirmidhī* 241; classified as *Ḍaʿīf* by al-Tirmidhī but as *Ḥasan* by al-Albānī)

l. Doors of Heaven are opened before Ẓuhr

ʿAbdullāh ibn al-Sāʾib (ﷺ) reported: The Messenger of Allah (ﷺ) would pray four cycles after the decline of the sun before noon prayer and he would say:

إِنَّهَا سَاعَةٌ تُفْتَحُ فِيهَا أَبْوَابُ السَّمَاءِ وَأُحِبُّ أَنْ يَصْعَدَ لِي فِيهَا عَمَلٌ صَالِحٌ

"Verily, there is an hour in which the gates of heaven are opened and I love that my good deeds ascend during it." (*Sunan al-Tirmidhī* 478, *Ṣaḥīḥ*)

m. Whoever prays the five daily prayers and abstains from major sins

ʿAbdullāh ibn ʿAmr (ﷺ) reported: The Prophet (ﷺ) ascended the pulpit and said:

لَا أُقْسِمُ، لَا أُقْسِمُ، لَا أُقْسِمُ

"I take an oath (by Allah)! I take an oath (by Allah)! I take an oath (by Allah)!" He (ﷺ) then descended therefrom and said:

أَبْشِرُوا أَبْشِرُوا، إنه مَنْ صَلَّى الصَّلَوَاتِ الْخَمْسَ وَاجْتَنَبَ الْكَبَائِرَ دَخَلَ مِنْ أَبْوَابِ الْجَنَّةِ شَاءَ

"Rejoice! Rejoice! Verily, whoever performs the five prayers and avoids the major sins will enter Jannah from whichever gate he wishes." (*al-Muʿjam al-Kabīr lil-Ṭabarānī* 13/8, *Ḥasan* according to al-Albānī)

Bāb al-Ṣalāh, the gate of prayer so divine,
Where fervent hearts to Allah incline.

With *wuḍū*'s purity, the key we wield,
Unlocking gates of *Jannah*, our faith revealed.

Taḥiyyat al-Wuḍūʾ, a humble prayer's grace,
Leads to *Jannah*'s castle, a heavenly place.

Six *rakʿāt* after *Maghrib*, devotion's light,
Illuminate our path to *Jannah*'s sight.

Twelve *nafl rakʿah*, in daylight's gleam,
Earn us a house in Paradise—the dream!

Recite *Āyat al-Kursī*, after prayer's embrace,
To enter into *Jannah*, Allah's boundless grace.

The *adhān*'s words, repeated and sincere,
Open *Jannah*'s gate and surely bring us near.

Four *Sunnah* of *Ẓuhr*, a shield and guard,
Against *Jahannam*'s flames, our prayer stands hard.

Tahajjud prayer, darkness' quiet hush,
Guides us to *Jannah*, where virtues thusly gush.

Freedom from hypocrisy, from Hellfire's chain,
Through prayer's devotion, eternal gain.

Before *Ẓuhr*'s call, the door of *Jannah* shines,
A glimpse of Paradise, in those blessed times.

For those who pray, their faith's unwavering flame,
Jannah's gates await, their righteous claim.

CHAPTER

Three

BĀB AL-JIHĀD

GATE OF JIHAD

ٱلَّذِينَ ءَامَنُوا۟ وَهَاجَرُوا۟ وَجَٰهَدُوا۟ فِى سَبِيلِ ٱللَّهِ بِأَمْوَٰلِهِمْ وَأَنفُسِهِمْ أَعْظَمُ دَرَجَةً عِندَ ٱللَّهِ ۚ وَأُو۟لَٰٓئِكَ هُمُ ٱلْفَآئِزُونَ ﴿٢٠﴾

"Those who believe, who migrated and strove hard and fought in Allah's way with their wealth and lives, are far higher in degree with Allah. They are the successful." (*al-Tawbah*, 9:20)

إِنَّ ٱللَّهَ اشْتَرَى مِنَ ٱلْمُؤْمِنِيْنَ اَنفُسَهُمْ وَأَمْوَالَهُمْ بِأَنَّ لَهُمُ ٱلْجَنَّةَ يُقَاتِلُونَ فِي سَبِيلِ ٱللَّهِ فَيَقْتُلُونَ وَيُقْتَلُونَ ﴿١١١﴾

"Indeed, Allah has purchased from the believers their lives and their properties [in exchange] for that they will have *Jannah*. They fight in the cause of Allah, so they kill and are killed." (*al-Tawbah*, 9:111)

وَلَا تَقُولُوا۟ لِمَن يُقْتَلُ فِى سَبِيلِ ٱللَّهِ أَمْوَٰتٌۢ ۚ بَلْ أَحْيَآءٌ وَلَٰكِن لَّا تَشْعُرُونَ ﴿١٥٤﴾

"And do not say about those who are killed in the way of Allah, 'They are dead.' Rather, they are alive, but you perceive [it] not." (*al-Baqarah*, 2:154)

وَلا تَحْسَبَنَّ الَّذِينَ قُتِلُوا فِي سَبِيلِ اللَّهِ أَمْوَاتًا بَلْ أَحْيَاءٌ عِنْدَ رَبِّهِمْ يُرْزَقُونَ ﴿١٦٩﴾

"And never think of those who have been killed in the cause of Allah as dead. Rather, they are alive with their Lord, receiving provision." (*Āl ʿImrān*, 3:169)

a. ***Jannah has one hundred levels***

Abū Hurayrah (رضي الله عنه) said: The Messenger of Allah (ﷺ) said:

"In *Jannah* there are one hundred degrees which Allah has prepared for those who strive in jihad for the sake of Allah. The distance between each two degrees is like the distance between the heavens and the earth. When you ask Allah, ask Him for *al-Firdaws*, for it is the last part of *Jannah* and the highest part of *Jannah*, and at its top is the Throne of *al-Raḥmān*, and from it the rivers of *Jannah* gush forth."

(*Ṣaḥīḥ al-Bukhārī*, 7423)

b. *Jannah is under the shades of swords*

ʿAbdullāh ibn Abī Awfā (⌘) narrates: Allah's Messenger (⌘) said:

وَاعْلَمُوا أَنَّ الْجَنَّةَ تَحْتَ ظِلَالِ السُّيُوفِ

"Know that *Jannah* is under the shades of swords." (*Ṣaḥīḥ al-Bukhārī* 2818, *Ṣaḥīḥ Muslim* 1742)

c. *Sincerely asking for shahādah*

Sahl ibn Ḥanīf (⌘) narrates: The Prophet (⌘) said:

مَنْ سَأَلَ اللَّهَ الشَّهَادَةَ بِصِدْقٍ بَلَّغَهُ اللَّهُ مَنَازِلَ الشُّهَدَاءِ وَإِنْ مَاتَ عَلَى فِرَاشِهِ

"Whoever asks Allah sincerely for martyrdom, Allah will cause him to reach the status of the martyrs even if he dies in his bed." (*Ṣaḥīḥ Muslim* 1909)

d. *Seven blessings for a martyr*

Al-Miqdām ibn Maʿdī Karib (⌘) narrates: The Prophet (⌘) said:

للشهيدِ عندَ اللهِ سبعُ خصالٍ : يُغفرُ لهُ في أوَّلِ دفعةٍ، ويَرى مقعدَهُ منَ الجنةِ، ويُجارُ مِنْ عذابِ القبرِ، ويأمنُ منَ الفزعِ الأكبرِ، ويُوضعُ على رأسِهِ تاجُ الوقارِ، الياقوتةُ منها خيرٌ منَ الدنيا وما فيها، ويُزوَّجُ اثنتينِ وسبعينَ زوجةً من الحورِ العينِ، ويُشفَّعُ في سبعينَ مِنْ أقاربِهِ

"The martyr has seven[1] blessings from Allah: 1) he is forgiven from the moment his blood is first shed; 2) he will be shown his place in *Jannah*; 3) he will be spared the trial of the grave; 4) he will be secure on the Day of the Greatest Terror (the Day of Judgement); 5) there

---

1 Some narrations of the *ḥadīth* state the number as six, nine, or ten. The author chose this *ḥadīth* due to its authenticity and numerous reporting.

will be placed on his head a crown of dignity, one ruby of which is better than this world and all that is in it; 6) he will be married to seventy-two of al-Ḥūr al-ʿAyn; and 7) he will be permitted to intercede for seventy of his relatives." (*Sunan al-Tirmidhī* 1663, *Ḥasan*, *Musnad Aḥmad* 17182, *Ibn Mājah* 2799)

e. ***A martyr wishes he can come back to earth***

Anas ibn Mālik (رضي الله عنه) narrates: The Prophet (ﷺ) said:

مَا أَحَدٌ يَدْخُلُ الْجَنَّةَ يُحِبُّ أَنْ يَرْجِعَ إِلَى الدُّنْيَا وَلَهُ مَا عَلَى الْأَرْضِ مِنْ شَيْءٍ إِلَّا الشَّهِيدُ يَتَمَنَّى أَنْ يَرْجِعَ إِلَى الدُّنْيَا فَيُقْتَلَ عَشْرَ مَرَّاتٍ لِمَا يَرَى مِنْ الْكَرَامَةِ

"No one who enters *Jannah* would like to return to the world, even if he could have everything on earth, except for the martyr. He will wish to return to the world and be killed ten more times, due to what he sees of dignity." (*Ṣaḥīḥ al-Bukhārī* 2662, *Ṣaḥīḥ Muslim* 1877)

f. ***A martyr's soul will be alive in green birds***

Kaʿb ibn Mālik (رضي الله عنه) narrates: The Messenger of Allah (ﷺ) said:

إِنَّ أَرْوَاحَ الشُّهَدَاءِ فِي طَيْرٍ خُضْرٍ تَعْلُقُ مِنْ ثَمَرِ الْجَنَّةِ أَوْ شَجَرِ الْجَنَّةِ

"Verily, the souls of martyrs are in green birds, hanging from the fruit of *Jannah*, or the trees of *Jannah*." (*Sunan al-Tirmidhī* 1641, *Ṣaḥīḥ*)

Masrūq (رحمه الله) reported: We asked ʿAbdullāh ibn Masʿūd (رضي الله عنه) about the verse:

وَلَا تَحْسَبَنَّ ٱلَّذِينَ قُتِلُوا۟ فِى سَبِيلِ ٱللَّهِ أَمْوَٰتًا ۚ بَلْ أَحْيَآءٌ عِندَ رَبِّهِمْ يُرْزَقُونَ ﴿١٦٩﴾

"And never think of those who have been killed in the cause of Allah as dead. Rather, they are alive with their Lord, receiving provision." (*Āl ʿImrān*, 3:169)

ʿAbdullāh (ﷺ) said: We asked the Prophet (ﷺ) about this verse, and he said:

أَرْوَاحُهُمْ فِي جَوْفِ طَيْرٍ خُضْرٍ لَهَا قَنَادِيلُ مُعَلَّقَةٌ بِالْعَرْشِ تَسْرَحُ مِنَ الْجَنَّةِ حَيْثُ شَاءَتْ ثُمَّ تَأْوِي إِلَى تِلْكَ الْقَنَادِيلِ فَاطَّلَعَ إِلَيْهِمْ رَبُّهُمُ اطِّلَاعَةً فَقَالَ هَلْ تَشْتَهُونَ شَيْئًا قَالُوا أَيَّ شَيْءٍ نَشْتَهِي وَنَحْنُ نَسْرَحُ مِنَ الْجَنَّةِ حَيْثُ شِئْنَا فَفَعَلَ ذَلِكَ بِهِمْ ثَلَاثَ مَرَّاتٍ فَلَمَّا رَأَوْا أَنَّهُمْ لَنْ يُتْرَكُوا مِنْ أَنْ يُسْأَلُوا قَالُوا يَا رَبِّ نُرِيدُ أَنْ تَرُدَّ أَرْوَاحَنَا فِي أَجْسَادِنَا حَتَّى نُقْتَلَ فِي سَبِيلِكَ مَرَّةً أُخْرَى فَلَمَّا رَأَى أَنْ لَيْسَ لَهُمْ حَاجَةٌ تُرِكُوا

"The souls of martyrs are alive in the bodies of green birds who have their nests in chandeliers hanging from the Throne of the Almighty. They eat the fruits of *Jannah* from wherever they wish, and they nestle among these chandeliers. Once their Lord cast a glance at them and He said: 'Do you want anything?' They said: 'What more could we desire? We eat the fruit of *Jannah* from wherever we wish.' Their Lord asked them the same question three times. When they saw that they will continue to be asked, they said: 'O Lord, we wish that You could return our souls to our bodies so that we could be martyred in Your way once again.' When Allah saw that they had no needs, He left them to enjoy." (*Ṣaḥīḥ Muslim* 1887)

g. *A martyr will be one of three people to enter first into Jannah*

Abū Hurayrah (ﷺ) reported: The Messenger of Allah (ﷺ) said:

عُرِضَ عَلَيَّ أَوَّلُ ثَلَاثَةٍ يَدْخُلُونَ الْجَنَّةَ شَهِيدٌ وَعَفِيفٌ مُتَعَفِّفٌ وَعَبْدٌ أَحْسَنَ عِبَادَةَ اللَّهِ وَنَصَحَ لِمَوَالِيهِ

"I was shown three people who will be among the first to enter *Jannah*: a martyr; one who refrains from begging; and a servant who worships Allah in the best manner and is sincere to his master." (*Sunan al-Tirmidhī* 1642, *Ḥasan*)

h. ***Three are guaranteed Jannah from Allah***

Abū Hurayrah (رضي الله عنه) reported: The Messenger of Allah (ﷺ) said:

ثَلاثَةٌ فِي ضَمَانِ اللَّهِ عَزَّ وَجَلَّ رَجُلٌ خَرَجَ مِنْ بَيْتِهِ إِلَى مَسْجِدٍ مِنْ مَسَاجِدِ اللَّهِ عَزَّ وَجَلَّ وَرَجُلٌ خَرَجَ غَازِيًا فِي سَبِيلِ اللَّهِ عَزَّ وَجَلَّ وَرَجُلٌ خَرَجَ حَاجًّا

"Three people have a guarantee from Allah the Almighty: a man who leaves his house to attend one of the mosques of Allah the Almighty; a man who goes out waging a campaign in the way of Allah the Almighty; and a man who goes out for the Hajj pilgrimage." (*Musnad al-Ḥumaydī* 1041, *Ṣaḥīḥ* according to al-Arnāʾūṭ)

Abū Umāmah (رضي الله عنه) reported: The Messenger of Allah (ﷺ) said:

ثَلاثَةٌ كُلُّهُمْ ضَامِنٌ عَلَى اللَّهِ إِنْ عَاشَ رُزِقَ وَكُفِيَ وَإِنْ مَاتَ أَدْخَلَهُ اللَّهُ الْجَنَّةَ مَنْ دَخَلَ بَيْتَهُ فَسَلَّمَ فَهُوَ ضَامِنٌ عَلَى اللَّهِ وَمَنْ خَرَجَ إِلَى الْمَسْجِدِ فَهُوَ ضَامِنٌ عَلَى اللَّهِ وَمَنْ خَرَجَ فِي سَبِيلِ اللَّهِ فَهُوَ ضَامِنٌ عَلَى اللَّهِ

"Three people have a guarantee from Allah. If he lives he will have provision to suffice him, and if he dies he will enter *Jannah*: one who enters and greets with peace has a guarantee from Allah; one who goes out to the *masjid* has a guarantee from Allah; and one who goes out in the way of Allah has a guarantee from Allah." (*Ṣaḥīḥ Ibn Ḥibbān* 504, *Ṣaḥīḥ* according to al-Mundhirī)

i. A sinful believer who fights in the way of Allah

ʿUtbah ibn ʿAbd al-Sulamī (ﷺ) narrates: The Messenger of Allah (ﷺ) said:

الْقَتْلى ثَلاثَةٌ : رَجُلٌ مُؤْمِنٌ قَاتَلَ بِنَفْسِهِ وَمَالِهِ فِي سَبِيلِ اللَّهِ حَتَّى إِذَا لَقِيَ الْعَدُوَّ قَاتَلَهُمْ حَتَّى يُقْتَلَ , فَذَلِكَ الشَّهِيدُ الْمُمْتَحَنُ فِي خَيْمَةِ اللَّهِ تَحْتَ عَرْشِهِ , لا يَفْضُلُهُ النَّبِيُّونَ إِلا بِدَرَجَةِ النُّبُوَّةِ ، وَرَجُلٌ مُؤْمِنٌ قَرَفَ عَلَى نَفْسِهِ مِنْ الذُّنُوبِ وَالْخَطَايَا جَاهَدَ بِنَفْسِهِ وَمَالِهِ فِي سَبِيلِ اللَّهِ حَتَّى إِذَا لَقِيَ الْعَدُوَّ قَاتَلَ حَتَّى يُقْتَلَ، مُحِيَتْ ذُنُوبُهُ وَخَطَايَاهُ , إِنَّ السَّيْفَ مَحَّاءُ الْخَطَايَا, وَأُدْخِلَ مِنْ أَيِّ أَبْوَابِ الْجَنَّةِ شَاءَ , فَإِنَّ لَهَا ثَمَانِيَةَ أَبْوَابٍ , وَلِجَهَنَّمَ سَبْعَةَ أَبْوَابٍ , وَبَعْضُهَا أَفْضَلُ مِنْ بَعْضٍ ، وَرَجُلٌ مُنَافِقٌ جَاهَدَ بِنَفْسِهِ وَمَالِهِ حَتَّى إِذَا لَقِيَ الْعَدُوَّ قَاتَلَ فِي سَبِيلِ اللَّهِ حَتَّى يُقْتَلَ فَإِنَّ ذَلِكَ فِي النَّارِ , السَّيْفُ لا يَمْحُو النِّفَاقَ

"A *mujāhid* can be of three types. A believer who fights in the way of Allah with his life and wealth, and when he encounters an enemy, he fights until he is killed. He is the purified (tested) martyr who will be in the tent under the Throne of Allah. The difference, in rank, between he and the prophets is due to their prophethood.

The second is the believer who has committed sins, then fights in the way of Allah with his life and wealth until he is killed. He will be cleansed from sins as wielding a sword in the way of Allah removes sins. He will be allowed to enter through any of the gates of *Jannah*. *Jannah* has eight gates, and *Jahannam* has seven gates, and some of them are lower than others.

The third is a hypocrite who fights in the path of Allah with life and wealth and gets killed. But he will go to *Jahannam* as the sword does not clean hypocrisy. (*Musnad Aḥmad* 17204, *Ḥasan* according to al-Albānī in *Ṣaḥīḥ al-Targhīb* 1370)

j. *Getting injured in the cause of Allah*

Muʿādh (ﷺ) reported: The Prophet (ﷺ) said:

مَنْ قاتل في سَبِيل الله من رَجُل مُسْلم فُوَاقَ نَاقَة، وجَبَتْ له الجنة، ومن جُرح جُرْحًا في سَبِيل الله أو نُكِبَ نَكْبَةً فإنها تَجِيء يوم القيامة كَأَغزَرِ ما كانت: لونُها الزَّعْفَرَانُ، وريُحها كالمِسك

"*Jannah* is guaranteed for any *muslim* who fights in the cause of Allah for the length of time between two milkings of a she-camel. Anyone who is wounded or injured in the cause of Allah, it will come on the Day of Judgment bleeding the most it ever bled, but its color will be like saffron and its fragrance will be like musk." (*Sunan Abū Dāwūd* 2541, *Sunan al-Tirmidhī* 1654 & 1657, *Sunan al-Nasāʾī* 3141, *Musnad Aḥmad* 22014, *Ṣaḥīḥ*)

Bāb al-Jihād, the gate where heroes stand,
In Allah's name, they march across the land.

Jannah's hundred levels, their noble quest,
Each step they take, in faith, they are blessed.

Under the shades of swords, they bravely fight,
Seeking martyrdom, their hearts alight.

Sincere in asking, *Shahādah* is their plea,
Their souls aflame for *Jannah*'s victory.

Seven blessings for a martyr's soul,
Their sacrifice, a purpose and a goal.

In *Jannah*'s bliss, they wish to return,
For the rewards of martyrs, they yearn.

As green birds, their souls take flight,
In Paradise's gardens, a radiant sight.

Among the first to enter Paradise's door:
A martyr's reward, forever they'll explore.

Three, Allah guarantees their heavenly grace,
Among them, the faithful who fight the righteous race.

Even a sinful heart, in Allah's name,
Who fights for justice, their soul aflame.

For those injured, wounded in Allah's way,
Their sacrifice is honoured, come what may.

Bāb al-Jihād, where valour's tales are spun,
In *Jannah*'s gates, their victory is truly won.

CHAPTER

Four

BĀB AL-ṢADAQAH

GATE OF CHARITY

لَن تَنَالُوا۟ ٱلْبِرَّ حَتَّىٰ تُنفِقُوا۟ مِمَّا تُحِبُّونَ ۚ وَمَا تُنفِقُوا۟ مِن شَىْءٍ فَإِنَّ ٱللَّهَ بِهِۦ عَلِيمٌ ﴿٩٢﴾

"By no means shall you attain *al-Birr* (piety, righteousness - here it means Allah's reward, i.e. *Jannah*), unless you spend (in Allah's cause) of that which you love; and whatever of good you spend, Allah knows it well." (*Āl ʿImrān*, 3:92)

Anas (ﷺ) added that when the above was revealed, Abū Ṭalḥah (ﷺ) stood up and went to the Messenger of Allah (ﷺ), and said: "O Messenger of Allah, Allah says: 'By no means shall you attain *al-Birr* unless you spend of that which you love...' The most beloved of my wealth to me is the garden of *Bayruḥāʾ* (also pronounced as *Bʾir-Ḥāʾ* (بئر حاء)), and I am giving it in charity to Allah, hoping to find reward for that with Allah. So dispose of it, O Messenger of Allah, as Allah shows you." The Messenger of Allah (ﷺ) said: "Bravo! That is a good deal, that is a good deal. I have heard what you said and I think that you should give it to your relatives." Abū Ṭalḥah said, "I will do that, O Messenger of Allah." So Abū Ṭalḥah shared it out among his relatives and cousins (sons of his paternal uncles). (*Ṣaḥīḥ al-Bukhārī* 1368, *Ṣaḥīḥ Muslim* 1664)

In *Masjid al-Nabawī*, there are markings on the tile of the floor which indicates where Abū Ṭalḥah's Garden of *Bayruḥāʾ* used to be. They are between gate 21 and gate 22, near the racks numbered 1241 and 1242.

a. ***Charity will give shade***

ʿUqbah ibn ʿĀmir (ﷺ) reported: The Messenger of Allah (ﷺ) said:

إِنَّ الصَّدَقَةَ لَتُطْفِئُ عَنْ أَهْلِهَا حَرَّ الْقُبُورِ وَإِنَّمَا يَسْتَظِلُّ الْمُؤْمِنُ يَوْمَ الْقِيَامَةِ فِي ظِلِّ صَدَقَتِهِ

"Verily, charity will protect people from the heat in their graves. Verily, only the believer will be shaded on the Day of Resurrection in the shade of his charity." (*al-Muʿjam al-Kabīr* 14223, *Shuʿab al-Īmān*

3076, *Ḥasan* according to al-Albānī)

b. ***A house will be built for him in Jannah***

ʿUthmān ibn ʿAffān (ﷺ) reported: The Messenger of Allah (ﷺ) said:

مَنْ بَنَى مَسْجِدًا لِلَّهِ بَنَى اللَّهُ لَهُ فِي الْجَنَّةِ مِثْلَهُ

"Whoever builds a *masjid* for Allah, Allah will build for him a house like it in *Jannah*." (*Ṣaḥīḥ al-Bukhārī* 439, *Ṣaḥīḥ Muslim* 533)

c. ***Virtue of charity inscribed on the Gate of Jannah***

Abū Umāmah (ﷺ) reported: The Messenger of Allah (ﷺ) said:

دَخَلَ رَجُلٌ الْجَنَّةَ فَرَأَى عَلَى بَابِهَا مَكْتُوبًا الصَّدَقَةُ بِعَشَرَةِ أَمْثَالِهَا وَالْقَرْضُ بِثَمَانِيَةَ عَشَرَ

"A man entered *Jannah* and he saw written upon its door: 'Charity is multiplied by ten times, and a good loan is multiplied by eighteen times.' " (*al-Muʿjam al-Kabīr* 7976, *Ḥasan* according to al-Albānī)

Anas ibn Mālik (ﷺ) reported: The Prophet (ﷺ) said:

رأيتُ ليلةَ أُسْرِيَ بي على بابِ الجنةِ مكتوبًا: الصدقةُ بعَشْرِ أمثالِها، والقَرْضُ بثمانيةَ عَشَرَ، فقلتُ يا جبريلُ: ما بالُ القَرْضِ أَفْضَلُ من الصدقةِ؟ قال: لِأَنَّ السائلَ يَسْأَلُ وعِنْدَهُ، والمُسْتَقْرِضُ لا يَسْتَقْرِضُ إلا من حاجةٍ

"I saw, on the Night of Ascension, written on the door of *Jannah*: 'Charity is multiplied by ten times, and a good loan is multiplied by eighteen times'. I asked Jibrīl (ﷺ): 'How is it that a good loan is better than charity?' Jibrīl replied: 'Because a begger asks, yet he may not be in need of it, while the borrower does not seek a loan except in (extreme) need.' " (*Sunan Ibn Mājah* 2431, *Ḍaʿīf*, *al-Jāmiʿ al-Ṣaghīr* 4369, *Ḥasan*)

d. Charity is a barrier from Jahannam

ʿĀʾishah (﷞) reported: The Messenger of Allah (ﷺ) said to her:

يَا عَائِشَةُ اسْتَتِرِي مِنَ النَّارِ وَلَوْ بِشِقِّ تَمْرَةٍ فَإِنَّهَا تَسُدُّ مِنَ الْجَائِعِ مَسَدَّهَا مِنَ الشَّبْعَانِ

"O ʿĀʾishah, set up a barrier from *Jahannam*, even with half of a date in charity, for it settles the hungry in place of the full." (*Musnad Aḥmad* 24501, *Ḥasan* according to Ibn Ḥajar)

e. Charity will make you enter Jannah in peace

ʿAbdullāh ibn Salām (﷞) narrates: The first thing I heard the Prophet (ﷺ) say when he arrived in *Madīnah*:

يَا أَيُّهَا النَّاسُ أَفْشُوا السَّلاَمَ وَأَطْعِمُوا الطَّعَامَ وَصِلُوا الأَرْحَامَ وَصَلُّوا بِاللَّيْلِ وَالنَّاسُ نِيَامٌ تَدْخُلُوا الْجَنَّةَ بِسَلاَمٍ

"O people, spread the *Salām*, feed the people, keep the ties of kinship, and pray during the night while others are asleep and you will enter *Jannah* in peace." (*Sunan Ibn Mājah* 3251, *Ṣaḥīḥ*, *Sunan al-Tirmidhī* 2485, *Ṣaḥīḥ*)

f. Removing something from the road will be rewarded with Jannah

Abū al-Dardāʾ (﷞) reported: The Prophet (ﷺ) said:

مَنْ زَحْزَحَ عَنْ طَرِيقِ الْمُسْلِمِينَ شَيْئًا يُؤْذِيهِمْ كَتَبَ اللَّهُ لَهُ بِهِ حَسَنَةً وَمَنْ كُتِبَ لَهُ عِنْدَهُ حَسَنَةٌ أَدْخَلَهُ اللَّهُ بِهَا الْجَنَّةَ

"Whoever pulls something out of the roads of the *muslims* that harms them, Allah will record a good deed for him. Whoever has a good deed written for him, Allah will admit him into *Jannah* by it." (*Musnad Aḥmad* 27479, *Ḥasan* according to al-Albānī)

Muʿādh ibn Jabal (ﷺ) reported: The Messenger of Allah (ﷺ) said:

مَنْ رَفَعَ حَجَرًا مِنَ الطَّرِيقِ كُتِبَتْ لَهُ حَسَنَةٌ وَمَنْ كَانَتْ لَهُ حَسَنَةٌ دَخَلَ الْجَنَّةَ

"Whoever removes a rock from the road, a good deed will be recorded for him. Whoever has done a good deed, he will enter *Jannah*." (*al-Muʿjam al-Kabīr* 16654, *Ḥasan* according to al-Albānī)

Muḥammad ibn Yaḥyā (ﷺ) reported: A man went out with Muʿādh ibn Jabal (ﷺ) and Muʿādh would not see anything harmful in the road but that he would move it to the side. When the man saw that, he would not pass by anything but that he would also move it to the side. Muʿādh said, "What made you do that?" The man said, "I saw you doing it." Muʿādh said, "You are right and have done well. Verily, whoever removes harmful things from the road of the *muslims* will have a good deed recorded for him, and whoever has a good deed recorded for him will enter *Jannah*." (*al-Adab li-Ibn Abī Shaybah* 111)

Abū Hurayrah (ﷺ) reported: The Prophet (ﷺ) said:

لَقَدْ رَأَيْتُ رَجُلاً يَتَقَلَّبُ فِي الْجَنَّةِ فِي شَجَرَةٍ قَطَعَهَا مِنْ ظَهْرِ الطَّرِيقِ كَانَتْ تُؤْذِي النَّاسَ

"I have seen a man enjoying himself in *Jannah* due to a tree in the road he cut down that used to harm people." (*Ṣaḥīḥ Muslim* 4751)

g. *The generous person is close to Allah, close to Jannah*

Abū Hurayrah (ﷺ) reported: The Prophet (ﷺ) said:

السَّخِيُّ قَرِيبٌ مِنْ اللَّهِ قَرِيبٌ مِنْ الْجَنَّةِ قَرِيبٌ مِنْ النَّاسِ بَعِيدٌ مِنْ النَّارِ وَالْبَخِيلُ بَعِيدٌ مِنْ اللَّهِ بَعِيدٌ مِنْ الْجَنَّةِ بَعِيدٌ مِنْ النَّاسِ قَرِيبٌ مِنْ النَّارِ وَلَجَاهِلٌ سَخِيٌّ أَحَبُّ إِلَى اللَّهِ عَزَّ وَجَلَّ مِنْ

عَالِمٍ بَخِيلٍ

"The generous one is near to Allah, near to *Jannah*, near to the people, and far from *Jahannam*. The miserly one is far from Allah, far from *Jannah*, far from the people, and near to *Jahannam*. An ignorant generous person is more beloved to Allah the Almighty than a stingy scholar." (*Sunan al-Tirmidhī* 1961, *Ṣaḥīḥ* according to al-Suyūṭī)

h. *Man forgiven for giving water to a dog*

Abū Hurayrah (ﷺ) reported: The Messenger of Allah (ﷺ) said:

بَيْنَمَا رَجُلٌ يَمْشِي بِطَرِيقٍ اشْتَدَّ عَلَيْهِ الْعَطَشُ فَوَجَدَ بِئْرًا فَنَزَلَ فِيهَا فَشَرِبَ ثُمَّ خَرَجَ فَإِذَا كَلْبٌ يَلْهَثُ يَأْكُلُ الثَّرَى مِنْ الْعَطَشِ فَقَالَ الرَّجُلُ لَقَدْ بَلَغَ هَذَا الْكَلْبَ مِنْ الْعَطَشِ مِثْلُ الَّذِي كَانَ بَلَغَ مِنِّي فَنَزَلَ الْبِئْرَ فَمَلَأَ خُفَّهُ مَاءً ثُمَّ أَمْسَكَهُ بِفِيهِ حَتَّى رَقِيَ فَسَقَى الْكَلْبَ فَشَكَرَ اللَّهُ لَهُ فَغَفَرَ لَهُ

"A man suffered from thirst while he was walking on a journey. When he found a well, he climbed down into it and drank from it. Then he came out and saw a dog lolling its tongue from thirst and licking the ground. The man said: 'This dog has suffered thirst just as I have suffered from it.' He climbed down into the well, filled his shoe with water, and held it in his mouth as he climbed up. Then he gave the dog a drink. Allah appreciated this deed, so He forgave him."

They said: "O Messenger of Allah, is there a reward for charity even for the animals?" The Prophet (ﷺ) said:

فِي كُلِّ كَبِدٍ رَطْبَةٍ أَجْرٌ

"Yes, in every creature with a moist liver is a reward for charity." (*Ṣaḥīḥ al-Bukhārī* 5663, *Ṣaḥīḥ Muslim* 2244)

i. ***Charity extinguishes the wrath of Allah***

Umm Salamah (﵂) reported: The Messenger of Allah (ﷺ) said:

صَنَائِعُ الْمَعْرُوفِ تَقِي مَصَارِعَ السَّوْءِ وَالصَّدَقَةُ خَفِيًّا تُطْفِئُ غَضَبَ الرَّبِّ وَصِلَةُ الرَّحِمِ زِيَادَةٌ
فِي الْعُمُرِ وَكُلُّ مَعْرُوفٍ صَدَقَةٌ وَأَهْلُ الْمَعْرُوفِ فِي الدُّنْيَا أَهْلُ الْمَعْرُوفِ فِي الآخِرَةِ وَأَهْلُ
الْمُنْكَرِ فِي الدُّنْيَا أَهْلُ الْمُنْكَرِ فِي الآخِرَةِ وَأَوَّلُ مَنْ يَدْخُلُ الْجَنَّةَ أَهْلُ الْمَعْرُوفِ

"Good works protect from evil fates. Charity in secret extinguishes the wrath of the Lord, maintaining family ties increases life span, and every good deed is charity. The people of good in the world are the people of good in the Hereafter, and the people of evil in the world are the people of evil in the Hereafter. And the first to enter *Jannah* are the people of good." (*al-Muʿjam al-Awsaṭ* 6252, *Ṣaḥīḥ* according to al-Albānī)

j. ***Charity admits one into Jannah***

Abū al-Dardāʾ (﵁) reported: The Messenger of Allah (ﷺ) said:

خَمْسٌ مَنْ جَاءَ بِهِنَّ مَعَ إِيمَانٍ دَخَلَ الْجَنَّةَ مَنْ حَافَظَ عَلَى الصَّلَوَاتِ الْخَمْسِ عَلَى وُضُوئِهِنَّ
وَرُكُوعِهِنَّ وَسُجُودِهِنَّ وَمَوَاقِيتِهِنَّ وَصَامَ رَمَضَانَ وَحَجَّ الْبَيْتَ إِنْ اسْتَطَاعَ إِلَيْهِ سَبِيلًا وَأَعْطَى
الزَّكَاةَ طَيِّبَةً بِهَا نَفْسُهُ وَأَدَّى الأَمَانَةَ

"Whoever comes with five deeds, along with faith, will enter *Jannah*: 1) one who preserves the five prayers, their ablution, their bowings, their prostrations, and their timings; 2) who fasts the month of *Ramaḍān;* 3) who performs the Hajj pilgrimage to the House if he can find a way; 4) who gives charity with a cheerful soul; and 5) one who fulfills the trust." (*Sunan Abī Dāwūd* 42)

k. ***Those whose last deeds are charity will enter Jannah***

Ḥudhayfah (﵁) reported: The Prophet (ﷺ) said:

مَنْ قَالَ لَا إِلَهَ إِلَّا اللَّهُ ابْتِغَاءَ وَجْهِ اللَّهِ خُتِمَ لَهُ بِهَا دَخَلَ الْجَنَّةَ وَمَنْ صَامَ يَوْمًا ابْتِغَاءَ وَجْهِ اللَّهِ خُتِمَ لَهُ بِهَا دَخَلَ الْجَنَّةَ وَمَنْ تَصَدَّقَ بِصَدَقَةٍ ابْتِغَاءَ وَجْهِ اللَّهِ خُتِمَ لَهُ بِهَا دَخَلَ الْجَنَّةَ

"Whoever declares there is no one worthy of worship but Allah, seeking the countenance of Allah as his last deed, he will enter *Jannah*. Whoever fasts a day, seeking the countenance of Allah as his last deed, he will enter *Jannah*. Whoever gives in charity, seeking the countenance of Allah as his last deed, he will enter *Jannah*." (*Musnad Aḥmad* 23324, *Ṣaḥīḥ li-ghayrihī* (authentic due to external evidence), according to al-Arnāʾūṭ)

Bāb al-Ṣadaqah, where hearts in kindness sway,
Charity's shade leads souls on their righteous way.

Each act of giving, like a house so fair,
In *Jannah*'s gardens, they find refuge there.

The gates of Paradise, with virtues lined,
Charity's grace, on each, is finely signed.

A barrier from *Jahannam*, strong and true,
Charity's power, as their recompense grew.

In peace, through charity, *Jannah*'s door awaits,
A soul enriched by what compassion creates.

Removing harm from the road, a noble feat,
Rewarded with *Jannah*, a blissful seat.

Generous hearts, to Allah, closely drawn,
In charity's light, their faith is brightly drawn.

For giving water to a humble dog one day,
A man's forgiveness paved *Jannah*'s way.

Charity's virtue, Allah's wrath does quell,
In His mercy's glow, all souls do dwell.

The ones whose final deeds are ones so kind,
In *Jannah*'s glory, they'll forever reside.

Bāb al-Ṣadaqah, where compassion blooms,
In *Jannah*'s embrace, their joy resumes.

في الجنة بابا يقال له الريان
يدخل منه الصائمون يوم
القيامة لا يدخل منه أحد

CHAPTER

Five

BĀB AL-RAYYĀN

GATE OF FASTING

a. ***Al-Rayyān is only for those who habitually fasted***

Sahl ibn Saʿd (ﷺ) reported: The Prophet (ﷺ) said:

إِنَّ فِي الْجَنَّةِ بَابًا يُقَالُ لَهُ الرَّيَّانُ يَدْخُلُ مِنْهُ الصَّائِمُونَ يَوْمَ الْقِيَامَةِ لَا يَدْخُلُ مِنْهُ أَحَدٌ غَيْرُهُمْ يُقَالُ أَيْنَ الصَّائِمُونَ فَيَقُومُونَ لَا يَدْخُلُ مِنْهُ أَحَدٌ غَيْرُهُمْ فَإِذَا دَخَلُوا أُغْلِقَ فَلَمْ يَدْخُلْ مِنْهُ أَحَدٌ

"Verily, there is a gate in *Jannah* called *al-Rayyān*, through which only those who fasted will enter on the Day of Resurrection. No one else will enter it along with them. It will be said: 'Where are those who fasted that they may enter?' When the last of them enter, it will be closed and no one else will go through it." (*Ṣaḥīḥ al-Bukhārī* 1797, *Ṣaḥīḥ Muslim* 1152)

b. ***All Gates of Jannah are opened in Ramaḍān***

Abū Hurayrah (ﷺ) reported: The Messenger of Allah (ﷺ) said:

إِذَا دَخَلَ شَهْرُ رَمَضَانَ فُتِّحَتْ أَبْوَابُ السَّمَاءِ وَغُلِّقَتْ أَبْوَابُ جَهَنَّمَ وَسُلْسِلَتِ الشَّيَاطِين

"When the month of *Ramaḍān* begins, the Gates of Heaven are opened, the gates of *Jahannam* are closed, and the devils are chained." (*Ṣaḥīḥ al-Bukhārī* 1899, *Ṣaḥīḥ Muslim* 1079)

c. ***Fasting is one of the main reasons to enter Jannah***

Abū Hurayrah (ﷺ) narrated:

A Bedouin came to the Prophet (ﷺ) and said, "Tell me of such a deed that will make me enter *Jannah* if I do it." The Prophet (ﷺ) said:

تَعْبُدُ اللَّهَ لاَ تُشْرِكُ بِهِ شَيْئًا، وَتُقِيمُ الصَّلاَةَ الْمَكْتُوبَةَ، وَتُؤَدِّى الزَّكَاةَ الْمَفْرُوضَةَ، وَتَصُومُ رَمَضَانَ

"Worship Allah, and do not associate anyone as partners with Him, offer the (five) prescribed obligatory prayers perfectly, pay the obligatory *zakāh*, and fast the month of *Ramaḍān*."

The bedouin said: "By Him in whose hands is my life, I will not do more than this." When he (the bedouin) left, the Prophet (ﷺ) said:

مَنْ سَرَّهُ أَنْ يَنْظُرَ إِلَى رَجُلٍ مِنْ أَهْلِ الْجَنَّةِ فَلْيَنْظُرْ إِلَى هَذَا

"Whoever likes to see a man of *Jannah*, then let him look at this man." (*Ṣaḥīḥ al-Bukhārī* 1397, *Ṣaḥīḥ Muslim* 14)

Jābir (ﷺ) narrates: That Nuʿmān ibn Qawqal came to the Prophet (ﷺ) and said:

يَا رَسُولَ اللَّهِ أَرَأَيْتَ إِذَا صَلَّيْتُ الْمَكْتُوبَةَ وَحَرَّمْتُ الْحَرَامَ وَأَحْلَلْتُ الْحَلاَلَ أَأَدْخُلُ الْجَنَّةَ فقال النَّبِيُّ صلى الله عليه وسلم: نَعَمْ

"Would I enter *Jannah* if I observe the obligatory prayers and deny myself that which is forbidden and treat that as lawful what has been made permissible (by the *Sharīʿah*)? The Prophet (ﷺ) replied: "Yes." (*Ṣaḥīḥ Muslim* 15)

d. ***Whoever fasts for the sake of Allah will enter Jannah***

Ḥudhayfah (ﷺ) reported: The Prophet (ﷺ) said:

مَنْ قَالَ لَا إِلَهَ إِلَّا اللَّهُ ابْتِغَاءَ وَجْهِ اللَّهِ خُتِمَ لَهُ بِهَا دَخَلَ الْجَنَّةَ وَمَنْ صَامَ يَوْمًا ابْتِغَاءَ وَجْهِ اللَّهِ خُتِمَ لَهُ بِهَا دَخَلَ الْجَنَّةَ وَمَنْ تَصَدَّقَ بِصَدَقَةٍ ابْتِغَاءَ وَجْهِ اللَّهِ خُتِمَ لَهُ بِهَا دَخَلَ الْجَنَّةَ

"Whoever declares there is no one worthy of worship but Allah, seeking the countenance of Allah as his last deed, he will enter *Jannah*. Whoever fasts a day, seeking the countenance of Allah as his last deed, he will enter *Jannah*. Whoever gives in charity, seeking the countenance of Allah as his last deed, he will enter *Jannah*." (*Musnad Aḥmad* 23324, *Ṣaḥīḥ li-ghayrihī* (authentic due to external evidence), according to al-Arnāʾūṭ)

e. *Whoever dies while fasting will enter Jannah*

ʿĀʾishah (﵂) narrates: The Prophet (ﷺ) said:

إِنَّمَا الْأَعْمَالُ بِالْخَوَاتِيمِ

"Verily, the (results of) deeds done depend upon the last actions." (*Ṣaḥīḥ Ibn Ḥibbān* 340, *Ṣaḥīḥ*)

A similar report is narrated by Sahl ibn Saʿd al-Sāʿidī (﵁) in a longer narration in which the Prophet (ﷺ) said:

إِنَّ الْعَبْدَ لَيَعْمَلُ فِيمَا يَرَى النَّاسُ عَمَلَ أَهْلِ الْجَنَّةِ، وَإِنَّهُ لَمِنْ أَهْلِ النَّارِ، وَيَعْمَلُ فِيمَا يَرَى النَّاسُ عَمَلَ أَهْلِ النَّارِ وَهْوَ مِنْ أَهْلِ الْجَنَّةِ، وَإِنَّمَا الأَعْمَالُ بِخَوَاتِيمِهَا

"A person may do deeds that seem to the people as the deeds of the people of *Jannah* while in fact, he is from the dwellers of the (Hell) Fire. Similarly, a person may do deeds that seem to the people as the deeds of the people of the (Hell) Fire while in fact, he is from the dwellers of *Jannah*. Verily, the (results of) deeds done depend upon the last actions." (*Ṣaḥīḥ al-Bukhārī* 6493)

f. *There are two pleasures a fasting person will get*

Abū Hurayrah (﵁) reported: The Messenger of Allah (ﷺ) said:

كُلُّ عَمَلِ ابْنِ آدَمَ لَهُ إِلاَّ الصِّيَامَ فَإِنَّهُ لِي وَأَنَا أَجْزِي بِهِ وَالصِّيَامُ جُنَّةٌ وَإِذَا كَانَ يَوْمُ صَوْمِ أَحَدِكُمْ فَلاَ يَرْفُثْ وَلاَ يَصْخَبْ فَإِنْ سَابَّهُ أَحَدٌ أَوْ قَاتَلَهُ فَلْيَقُلْ إِنِّي امْرُؤٌ صَائِمٌ وَالَّذِي نَفْسُ مُحَمَّدٍ بِيَدِهِ لَخُلُوفُ فَمِ الصَّائِمِ أَطْيَبُ عِنْدَ اللَّهِ مِنْ رِيحِ الْمِسْكِ لِلصَّائِمِ فَرْحَتَانِ يَفْرَحُهُمَا

إِذَا أَفْطَرَ فَرِحَ وَإِذَا لَقِيَ رَبَّهُ فَرِحَ بِصَوْمِهِ

"Allah the Almighty said: 'Every deed of the son of Ādam is for him, except for fasting. It is for Me and I will reward it.' Fasting is a shield so when one of you fasts, he should not be obscene or rowdy. If someone insults him or fights him, let him say: 'Indeed, I am fasting.' By the One in whose hand is the soul of Muhammad, the breath coming from the mouth of a fasting person is more pleasant to Allah than the scent of musk. The fasting person will have two moments of joy: when he breaks his fast he is joyful, and when he meets his Lord he will be joyful for his fasting." (*Ṣaḥīḥ al-Bukhārī* 1904, *Ṣaḥīḥ Muslim* 1151)

g. *Fasting is protection from Jahannam*

ʿUthmān ibn Abī al-ʿĀṣ (ﷺ) reported: The Messenger of Allaḥ (ﷺ) said:

الصِّيَامُ جُنَّةٌ مِنْ النَّارِ كَجُنَّةِ أَحَدِكُمْ مِنْ الْقِتَالِ

"Fasting is a shield from *Jahannam*, just like a shield of yours in battle." (*Sunan Ibn Mājah* 1639, *Ṣaḥīḥ* according to al-Albānī)

Abū Umāmah (ﷺ) reported: The Prophet (ﷺ) said:

مَنْ صَامَ يَوْمًا فِي سَبِيلِ اللَّهِ جَعَلَ اللَّهُ بَيْنَهُ وَبَيْنَ النَّارِ خَنْدَقًا كَمَا بَيْنَ السَّمَاءِ وَالْأَرْضِ

"Whoever fasts a day in the way of Allah, Allah will make a trench between him and *Jahannam* whose distance is like that between the heavens and the earth." (*Sunan al-Tirmidhī* 1624, *Ṣaḥīḥ* according to al-Albānī)

Abū Hurayrah (ﷺ) reported: The Messenger of Allah (ﷺ) said:

مَنْ صَامَ يَوْمًا فِي سَبِيلِ اللَّهِ عَزَّ وَجَلَّ زَحْزَحَ اللَّهُ وَجْهَهُ عَنْ النَّارِ بِذَلِكَ الْيَوْمِ سَبْعِينَ خَرِيفًا

"Whoever fasts a day in the way of Allah the Almighty, by that day Allah will deliver his face from *Jahannam* a distance of seventy autumns of travel." (*Sunan al-Nasāʾī* 2244, *Ṣaḥīḥ* according to al-Albānī)

ʿUqbah ibn ʿĀmir (ﷺ) reported: The Messenger of Allah (ﷺ) said:

مَنْ صَامَ يَوْمًا فِي سَبِيلِ اللَّهِ عَزَّ وَجَلَّ بَاعَدَ اللَّهُ مِنْهُ جَهَنَّمَ مَسِيرَةَ مِائَةِ عَامٍ

"Whoever fasts a day in the way of Allah the Almighty, Allah will distance him from *Jahannam* by a measure of one hundred years of travel." (*Sunan al-Nasāʾī* 2254, *Ḥasan* according to al-Albānī)

h. His thirst will be quenched on the Day of Judgement

Abū Mūsā al-Ashʿarī (ﷺ) narrates:

إنَّ اللهَ قَضَى على نفسِهِ أنَّ مَنْ عَطَّشَ نفسَهُ للَّهِ في يَوْمٍ حارٍّ ؛ كان حَقًّا على اللهِ أنْ يَرْوِيَهُ يومَ القيامةِ

"Allah had decreed upon Himself that whomever is thirsty (due to fasting) for Allah's sake on a hot day, it is incumbent upon Allah to quench him on the Day of Judgment." (al-Bayhaqī in *Shuʿab al-Īmān*, *Ḍaʿīf* according to al-Albānī in *Ḍaʿīf al-Targhīb* 578)

Kaʿb (ﷺ) said that Allah the Most High said to Prophet Mūsā (ﷺ): "I have made it incumbent upon Myself for whomever is thirsty for My sake that I will quench his thirst on the Day of Resurrection." (Ibn Rajab, *Laṭāʾif al-Maʿārif*, 322, and Ibn Abī al-Dunyā)

i. Fasting will intercede for you on the Day of Judgment

ʿAbdullāh ibn ʿĀmr (ﷺ) reported that the Messenger of Allah (ﷺ) said:

الصِّيَامُ وَالْقُرْآنُ يَشْفَعَانِ لِلْعَبْدِ يَوْمَ الْقِيَامَةِ يَقُولُ الصِّيَامُ أَيْ رَبِّ مَنَعْتُهُ الطَّعَامَ وَالشَّهَوَاتِ بِالنَّهَارِ فَشَفِّعْنِي فِيهِ وَيَقُولُ الْقُرْآنُ مَنَعْتُهُ النَّوْمَ بِاللَّيْلِ فَشَفِّعْنِي فِيهِ قَالَ فَيُشَفَّعَانِ

"Fasting and the *Qurʾan* will intercede for the servant on the Day of Resurrection. Fasting will say: 'O Lord, I prevented him from food and drink during the day, so let me intercede for him.' The *Qurʾan* will say: 'O Lord, I prevented him from sleeping during the night, so let me intercede for him.' Thus, they will both intercede for him." (*Musnad Aḥmad* 6589, *Ṣaḥīḥ* according to Aḥmad Shākir, *Musnad Aḥmad* 6626, *Ṣaḥīḥ* according to al-Albānī)

j. Allah has people He redeems from Jahannam on every single day and night

Jābir (ﷺ) reported: The Messenger of Allah (ﷺ) said:

إِنَّ لِلَّهِ عِنْدَ كُلِّ فِطْرٍ عُتَقَاءَ وَذَلِكَ فِي كُلِّ لَيْلَةٍ

"Verily, Allah has people He redeems at the time of breaking fast, and that is during every night." (*Sunan Ibn Mājah* 1643, *Ṣaḥīḥ* according to al-Albānī)

Abū Saʿīd al-Khudrī (ﷺ) reported: The Messenger of Allah (ﷺ) said:

إِنَّ لِلَّهِ عُتَقَاءَ فِي كُلِّ يَوْمٍ وَلَيْلَةٍ يعني في رمضان لِكُلِّ عَبْدٍ مِنْهُمْ دَعْوَةٌ مُسْتَجَابَةٌ

"Verily, Allah has people He redeems in every day and night of *Ramaḍān*, and every servant among them has a supplication that will be answered." (*Musnad Aḥmad* 7450, *Ṣaḥīḥ* according to al-Arnā'ūṭ)

Abū Hurayrah (ﷺ) reported: The Messenger of Allah (ﷺ) said:

إِذَا كَانَ أَوَّلُ لَيْلَةٍ مِنْ شَهْرِ رَمَضَانَ صُفِّدَتْ الشَّيَاطِينُ وَمَرَدَةُ الْجِنِّ وَغُلِّقَتْ أَبْوَابُ النَّارِ فَلَمْ يُفْتَحْ مِنْهَا بَابٌ وَفُتِّحَتْ أَبْوَابُ الْجَنَّةِ فَلَمْ يُغْلَقْ مِنْهَا بَابٌ وَيُنَادِي مُنَادٍ يَا بَاغِيَ الْخَيْرِ أَقْبِلْ وَيَا بَاغِيَ الشَّرِّ أَقْصِرْ وَلِلَّهِ عُتَقَاءُ مِنْ النَّارِ وَذَلِكَ كُلُّ لَيْلَةٍ

"On the first night of the month of *Ramaḍān*, the devils are chained and the jinn are restrained, the gates of *Jahannam* are closed and none of its gates are opened, the Gates of *Jannah* are opened and none of its gates are closed, and a heavenly caller announces: 'O seeker of good, come near! O seeker of evil, stop short!' Allah has those He saves from *Jahannam*, and that is during every night." (*Sunan al-Tirmidhī* 682, *Ḥasan* according to al-Albānī)

k. *Every single day and night the muslim has a duʿā that is accepted*

Abū Hurayrah (ﷺ) narrated: The Messenger of Allah (ﷺ) said:

ثَلَاثَةٌ لَا تُرَدُّ دَعْوَتُهُمْ الصَّائِمُ حَتَّى يُفْطِرَ وَالْإِمَامُ الْعَادِلُ وَدَعْوَةُ الْمَظْلُومِ يَرْفَعُهَا اللَّهُ فَوْقَ الْغَمَامِ وَيَفْتَحُ لَهَا أَبْوَابَ السَّمَاءِ وَيَقُولُ الرَّبُّ وَعِزَّتِي لَأَنْصُرَنَّكِ وَلَوْ بَعْدَ حِينٍ

"There are three whose *duʿā* is not rejected: a just ruler, the fasting person when he breaks his fast, and the prayer of the oppressed person. It rises above the clouds and the Gates of Heaven are opened for it, and the Lord, may He be glorified, says, 'By My Glory I will answer you even if it is after a while.' " (*Sunan al-Tirmidhī* 2525, *Ṣaḥīḥ*)

Abū Saʿīd al-Khudrī (﵁) reported: The Messenger of Allah (ﷺ) said:

إِنَّ لِلَّهِ عُتَقَاءَ فِي كُلِّ يَوْمٍ وَلَيْلَةٍ يعني في رمضان لِكُلِّ عَبْدٍ مِنْهُمْ دَعْوَةٌ مُسْتَجَابَةٌ

"Verily, Allah has people He redeems in every day and night of *Ramaḍān*, and every servant among them has a supplication that will be answered." (*Musnad Aḥmad* 7450, *Ṣaḥīḥ* according to al-Arnāʾūṭ, *Musnad Aḥmad* 7401, *Ṣaḥīḥ* according to al-Albānī in *Ṣaḥīḥ al-Jāmiʿ* 2169)

Bāb al-Rayyān, gate of fasting's grace,
For those who steadfastly seek *Jannah*'s embrace.

Habitual fasting was their noble way,
To Rayyān's door, they'll hasten and obey.

Ramaḍān's arrival, gates of *Jannah* wide,
In fasting's devotion, hearts are purified.

Fasting: a key to *Jannah*'s vast terrain,
A path to Paradise, where blessings reign.

For Allah's sake, they fast, their hearts alight,
In *Jannah*'s gardens, they'll find their light.

Those who pass away, fasting's sacred call,
In *Jannah*'s realms, their souls stand tall.

Two pleasures they embrace, with love and care,
Breaking their fast, and *Jannah*'s bliss to share.

Fasting shields from *Jahannam*'s fiery might,
A refuge strong, in Allah's guiding light.

On Judgment Day, their thirst shall disappear,
For faithful hearts, salvation's water's near.

Fasting intercedes, on Judgment's grand display,
A voice for the devout, on the ultimate day.

Each day and night, Allah's mercy shines,
Redeems souls and frees them—a mercy most divine!

A *duʿā* accepted, in the dark and bright,
For *muslims* who, in faith, seek Allah's light.

Bāb al-Rayyān, a path to *Jannah*'s grace,
In fasting's beauty, we find our rightful place.

CHAPTER

Six

AL-BĀB AL-AYMAN

THE RIGHT GATE

This door is reserved for the entry of such people who are saved from reckoning and punishment. It is also known as *Bāb al-Mutawakkilīn* – the gate of those who rely upon Allah – according to the *ḥadīth* narrated by Ibn ʿAbbās (ﷺ).

Abū Hurayrah (ﷺ) reported: The Messenger of Allah (ﷺ) said:

يُقَالُ يَوْمَ الْقِيَامَةِ يَا مُحَمَّدُ أَدْخِلْ مِنْ أُمَّتِكَ مَنْ لَا حِسَابَ عَلَيْهِمْ مِنَ الْبَابِ الْأَيْمَنِ مِنْ أَبْوَابِ الْجَنَّةِ وَهُمْ شُرَكَاءُ النَّاسِ فِيمَا سِوَى ذَلِكَ مِنَ الْأَبْوَابِ

"It will be said on the Day of Resurrection: 'O Muhammad! Admit those from your nation, who will not be held to account, through the right gate among the gates of *Jannah*, yet they will still share the other gates with the rest of the people'." (*Ṣaḥīḥ al-Bukhārī* 4712, *Ṣaḥīḥ Muslim* 194)

a. Seventy thousand will enter Jannah without any reckoning

Ibn ʿAbbās (ﷺ) narrated: The Prophet (ﷺ) said:

عُرِضَتْ عَلَيَّ الْأُمَمُ فَجَعَلَ النَّبِيُّ وَالنَّبِيَّانِ يَمُرُّونَ مَعَهُمْ الرَّهْطُ وَالنَّبِيُّ لَيْسَ مَعَهُ أَحَدٌ حَتَّى رُفِعَ لِي سَوَادٌ عَظِيمٌ قُلْتُ مَا هَذَا أُمَّتِي هَذِهِ قِيلَ بَلْ هَذَا مُوسَى وَقَوْمُهُ قِيلَ انْظُرْ إِلَى الْأُفُقِ فَإِذَا سَوَادٌ يَمْلَأُ الْأُفُقَ ثُمَّ قِيلَ لِي انْظُرْ هَا هُنَا وَهَا هُنَا فِي آفَاقِ السَّمَاءِ فَإِذَا سَوَادٌ قَدْ مَلَأَ الْأُفُقَ قِيلَ هَذِهِ أُمَّتُكَ وَيَدْخُلُ الْجَنَّةَ مِنْ هَؤُلَاءِ سَبْعُونَ أَلْفًا بِغَيْرِ حِسَابٍ

"I was shown the nations, and some Prophets passed by with a few followers, and some Prophets passed by with no followers. Then I was shown a great multitude, and I said: 'What is this? Is this my *Ummah*?' It was said: 'No, this is Mūsā (ﷺ) and his people'. It was said: 'Look at the horizon'. There I saw a huge multitude filling the horizon. And it was said: 'Look there, and there, on the horizons of the sky'. There was a multitude filling the horizons. It was said: 'This is your *Ummah* and, of them, seventy thousand will enter *Jannah* without being brought to account.' "

Then he (the Prophet (ﷺ)) went inside, without explaining further. The people started to discuss what he had said, saying: 'We are the ones who have believed in Allah and followed His Messenger: we are they'; or, 'It is our children who were born in *Islām* whilst we were born in *Jāhiliyyah*.' The Prophet (ﷺ) heard about what was being said, so he came out and said:

هُمُ الَّذِينَ لاَ يَسْتَرْقُونَ وَلاَ يَتَطَيَّرُونَ وَلاَ يَكْتَوُونَ وَعَلَى رَبِّهِمْ يَتَوَكَّلُونَ

"They are the ones who do not seek *Ruqyah*, do not believe in bad omens and do not use cauterization; but rather they put their trust in their Lord."

ʿUkkāshah ibn Miḥṣan (رضي الله عنه) stood up and said: "Pray to Allah to make me one of them!" He (the Prophet (ﷺ)) said: "O Allah, make him one of them." Then another man stood up and said: "Pray to Allah to make me one of them." He (ﷺ) said: "ʿUkkāshah has beaten you to it." (*Ṣaḥīḥ al-Bukhārī* 5378)

b. *Their faces will be like the full moon*

Sahl ibn Saʿd (رضي الله عنه) narrated: The Prophet (ﷺ) said:

لَيَدْخُلَنَّ الجَنَّةَ مِن أُمَّتي سَبْعُونَ ألْفًا، أوْ سَبْعُ مِئَةِ ألْفٍ – شَكَّ في أحَدِهِما – مُتَماسِكِينَ، آخِذٌ بَعْضُهُمْ بِبَعْضٍ، حتَّى يَدْخُلَ أوَّلُهُمْ وآخِرُهُمُ الجَنَّةَ، ووُجُوهُهُمْ علَى ضَوْءِ القَمَرِ لَيْلَةَ البَدْرِ

"Seventy thousand or seven hundred thousand (one of the narrators was not sure) of my *Ummah* will enter *Jannah*, holding each other and the first of them will not enter until the last of them do so. And their faces will be like the moon on the night when it is full." (*Ṣaḥīḥ al-Bukhārī* 6543)

In the version in *Ṣaḥīḥ Muslim* it states:

"... then the believers will be saved and the first group to be saved will have faces like the moon when it is full; [they will be] seventy thousand, who will not be brought to account. Then will come those who shine like the stars in the sky..." (*Ṣaḥīḥ Muslim* 191)

c. *Good news for every believer*

Abū Umāmah (ﷺ) reported: The Prophet (ﷺ) said:

وَعَدَنِي رَبِّي أَنْ يُدْخِلَ الْجَنَّةَ مِنْ أُمَّتِي سَبْعِينَ أَلْفًا لَا حِسَابَ عَلَيْهِمْ وَلَا عَذَابَ مَعَ كُلِّ أَلْفٍ سَبْعُونَ أَلْفًا وَثَلَاثُ حَثَيَاتٍ مِنْ حَثَيَاتِهِ

"My Lord has promised me that seventy thousand from my nation will enter *Jannah* without reckoning or punishment. Along with every thousand are seventy thousand more, and three more immeasurable groups of His choosing." (*Sunan al-Tirmidhī* 2437, *Ṣaḥīḥ* according to al-Albānī)

d. *Ummah of Prophet Muhammad (ﷺ) will be half of the inhabitants of Jannah*

Abū Saʿīd al-Khudrī (ﷺ) narrated: The Prophet (ﷺ) said:

وَالَّذِي نَفْسِي بِيَدِهِ إِنِّي لَأَطْمَعُ أَنْ تَكُونُوا رُبُعَ أَهْلِ الْجَنَّةِ

"By the One in whose hand is my soul, I hope you will be a quarter of the people of *Jannah*."

They (the *Ṣaḥābah*) praised Allah and exalted Him, then the Prophet (ﷺ) said:

وَالَّذِي نَفْسِي بِيَدِهِ إِنِّي لَأَطْمَعُ أَنْ تَكُونُوا ثُلُثَ أَهْلِ الْجَنَّةِ

"By the One in whose hand is my soul, I hope you will be a third of the people of *Jannah*."

They (the *Ṣaḥābah*) praised Allah and exalted Him, then the Prophet (ﷺ) said:

وَالَّذِي نَفْسِي بِيَدِهِ إِنِّي لأَطْمَعُ أَنْ تَكُونُوا شَطْرَ أَهْلِ الْجَنَّةِ إِنَّ مَثَلَكُمْ فِي الأُمَمِ كَمَثَلِ الشَّعْرَةِ الْبَيْضَاءِ فِي جِلْدِ الثَّوْرِ الأَسْوَدِ أَوْ كَالرَّقْمَةِ فِي ذِرَاعِ الْحِمَارِ

"By the One in whose hand is my soul, I hope you will be half of the people of *Jannah*. Verily, your likeness among the nations is that of a white hair on the skin of a black ox or a strip on the foreleg of a donkey." (*Ṣaḥīḥ Muslim* 222)

e. *Eighty out of one hundred and twenty rows will be for this Ummah*

Buraydah (رضي الله عنه) narrates: The Prophet (ﷺ) said:

أَهْلُ الْجَنَّةِ عِشْرُونَ وَمِائَةُ صَفٍّ ثَمَانُونَ مِنْهَا مِنْ هَذِهِ الأُمَّةِ وَأَرْبَعُونَ مِنْ سَائِرِ الأُمَمِ

"The people of *Jannah* are one hundred and twenty rows, of which eighty are from this *Ummah* and the other forty from all the other nations." (*Sunan al-Tirmidhī* 2546, *Ḥasan*)

Bāb al-Ayman, where grace and blessings flow,
For seventy thousand, the Gardens be aglow.

They'll enter *Jannah*, no reckoning to endure,
Their faces radiant, like the moon so pure.

Good news for every believer's soul,
In *Jannah*'s embrace, their hearts made whole.

Prophet Muhammad's *Ummah*, a blessed sight,
Half of *Jannah*'s dwellers, in heavenly light.

Eighty rows of one hundred twenty, we'll find,
Reserved for this *Ummah*, the faithful and kind.

Bāb al-Ayman, a gate of hope and cheer,
For those who believe, Paradise draws near.

والذاكرين الله كثيرا والذاكرات أعد الله لهم مغفرة وأجرا عظيما

CHAPTER

Seven

BĀB AL-DHIKR

GATE OF DIVINE REMEMBRANCE[2]

2 According to Ibn Ḥajar al-ʿAsqalānī and Imam al-Tirmidhī (ؒ).

Those who excessively remember Allah will be admitted through this gate.

Al-Mughīrah ibn Shuʿbah (ﷺ) reported: The Messenger of Allah (ﷺ) said:

لَا شَخْصَ أَغْيَرُ مِنَ اللهِ وَلَا شَخْصَ أَحَبُّ إِلَيْهِ الْعُذْرُ مِنَ اللهِ مِنْ أَجْلِ ذَلِكَ بَعَثَ اللهُ الْمُرْسَلِينَ مُبَشِّرِينَ وَمُنْذِرِينَ وَلَا شَخْصَ أَحَبُّ إِلَيْهِ الْمِدْحَةُ مِنَ اللهِ مِنْ أَجْلِ ذَلِكَ وَعَدَ اللهُ الْجَنَّةَ

"No one has a greater sense of honour than Allah. No one loves to allow excuses more than Allah. For this reason, He sent the Messengers to give glad tidings and warnings. No one loves to be praised more than Allah on account of what Allah has promised of *Jannah*." (*Ṣaḥīḥ Muslim* 1499)

a. The best people to Allah on the Day of Judgment

Abū Saʿīd al-Khudrī (ﷺ) narrates: The Prophet (ﷺ) was asked:

"Which of the servants of Allah is best in rank before Allah on the Day of Resurrection?" He said:

الذَّاكرونَ اللَّهَ كثيرًا

"The ones who remember him much." I said: "O Messenger of Allah, what about the fighter in the way of Allah?" He answered:

لو ضربَ بسيفِهِ في الكفَّارِ والمشرِكينَ حتَّى ينْكسرَ ويختضبَ دمًا لَكانَ الذَّاكرونَ اللَّهَ كثيرًا أفضلَ منهُ درجةً

"Even if he strikes the unbelievers and *mushrikīn* (polytheists) with his sword until it broke, and becomes red with their blood, truly those who do *dhikr* are better than him in rank." (*Musnad Aḥmad* 11720, *Sunan al-Tirmidhī* 3376, *Ḍaʿīf*, according al-Albānī)

Abū al-Dardā' (۝) narrates: The Prophet (۝) said:

$$\text{أَلاَ أُنَبِّئُكُمْ بِخَيْرٍ أَعْمَالِكُمْ وَأَزْكَاهَا عِنْدَ مَلِيكِكُمْ وَأَرْفَعِهَا فِي دَرَجَاتِكُمْ وَخَيْرٌ لَكُمْ مِنْ إِنْفَاقِ}$$
$$\text{الذَّهَبِ وَالْوَرِقِ وَخَيْرٌ لَكُمْ مِنْ أَنْ تَلْقَوْا عَدُوَّكُمْ فَتَضْرِبُوا أَعْنَاقَهُمْ وَيَضْرِبُوا أَعْنَاقَكُمْ}$$

"Should I not inform you of the best of your deed, and the purest of them with your Master, and the highest of them in your ranks, and what is better for you than spending gold and silver, and better for you than meeting your enemy and striking their necks, and they strike your necks?" They said: 'Of course.' He said:

$$\text{ذِكْرُ اللَّهِ تَعَالَى}$$

"The remembrance of Allah Most High."

[Then] Muʿādh ibn Jabal (۝) said: "There is nothing that brings more salvation from the punishment of Allah than the remembrance of Allah." (*Sunan al-Tirmidhī* 3377, *Ibn Mājah* 3072, *Musnad Aḥmad* 21750, *Ṣaḥīḥ* according to al-Albānī)

b. *The Ghanīmah of Dhikr of Allah is Jannah*

ʿAbdullāh ibn ʿAmr (۝) reported:

I said: "O Messenger of Allah, what are the spoils of gathering to remember Allah?" The Prophet (۝) said:

$$\text{غَنِيمَةُ مَجَالِسِ الذِّكْرِ الْجَنَّةُ}$$

"The spoils of the gatherings of remembrance is *Jannah*." (*Musnad Aḥmad* 6651, *Ḥasan* according to al-Haythamī)

c. Replying to the adhān will get you Jannah[3]

ʿUmar ibn al-Khaṭṭāb (ﷺ) reported: The Messenger of Allah (ﷺ) said:

إذا قالَ المُؤَذِّنُ: اللَّهُ أكْبَرُ اللَّهُ أكْبَرُ، فقالَ أحَدُكُمْ: اللَّهُ أكْبَرُ اللَّهُ أكْبَرُ، ثُمَّ قالَ: أشْهَدُ أنْ لا إلَهَ إلَّا اللَّهُ، قالَ: أشْهَدُ أنْ لا إلَهَ إلَّا اللَّهُ، ثُمَّ قالَ: أشْهَدُ أنَّ مُحَمَّدًا رَسولُ اللهِ قالَ: أشْهَدُ أنَّ مُحَمَّدًا رَسولُ اللهِ، ثُمَّ قالَ: حَيَّ علَى الصَّلاةِ، قالَ: لا حَوْلَ ولا قُوَّةَ إلَّا باللَّهِ، ثُمَّ قالَ: حَيَّ علَى الفَلاحِ، قالَ: لا حَوْلَ ولا قُوَّةَ إلَّا باللَّهِ، ثُمَّ قالَ: اللَّهُ أكْبَرُ اللَّهُ أكْبَرُ، قالَ: اللَّهُ أكْبَرُ اللَّهُ أكْبَرُ، ثُمَّ قالَ: لا إلَهَ إلَّا اللَّهُ، قالَ: لا إلَهَ إلَّا اللَّهُ مِن قَلْبِهِ دَخَلَ الجَنَّةَ

"When the caller to prayer says, 'Allah is the greatest, Allah is the greatest,' then let one of you say: 'Allah is the greatest, Allah is the greatest.' Then he says: 'I testify there is no god but Allah,' one says, 'I testify there is no god but Allah.' Then he says: 'I testify Muhammad is the Messenger of Allah,' one says, 'I testify Muhammad is the Messenger of Allah.' Then he says: 'Come to prayer,' one says, 'There is no power or might but in Allah.' Then he says: 'Come to salvation,' one says, 'There is no power or might but in Allah.' Then he says: 'Allah is the greatest, Allah is the greatest,' one says, 'Allah is the greatest, Allah is the greatest.' Then he says: 'There is no god but Allah,' one says, 'There is no god but Allah'—[whoever says all this] from his heart will enter *Jannah*." (*Ṣaḥīḥ Muslim* 385)

d. Planting your trees in Jannah

Ibn ʿUmar (ﷺ) reported: The Messenger of Allah (ﷺ) said:

أَكْثِرُوا مِنْ غَرْسِ الْجَنَّةِ فَإِنَّهُ عَذْبٌ مَاؤُهَا طَيِّبٌ تُرَابُهَا فَأَكْثِرُوا مِنْ غِرَاسِهَا لَا حَوْلَ وَلَا قُوَّةَ إِلَّا بِاللهِ

"Increase your plantings in *Jannah*, for its water is sweet and its soil

3 This was also mentioned in the Gate of Prayer section.

is clean. Its plantings are to say: 'There is no power nor might except through Allah.' " (*al-Muʿjam al-Kabīr* 13354, *Ḥasan* according to al-Suyūṭī)

Abū Hurayrah (ﷺ) reported: The Messenger of Allah (ﷺ) said:

أَفَلَا أَدُلُّكَ عَلَى كَلِمَةٍ مِنْ كَنْزِ الْجَنَّةِ مِنْ تَحْتِ الْعَرْشِ لَا قُوَّةَ إِلَّا بِاللهِ يَقُولُ أَسْلَمَ عَبْدِي وَاسْتَسْلَمَ

"Shall I not direct you to a word among the treasures of *Jannah* beneath the Throne? 'There is no strength except through Allah.' Allah says: 'My servant has completely surrendered to Me.' " (*Musnad Aḥmad* 7966, *Ḥasan* according to al-Arnāʾūṭ)

e. *Those who remember Allah enter Jannah laughing*

Jubayr ibn Nufayr (ﷺ) reported: Abū al-Dardāʾ (ﷺ) said:

إِنَّ الَّذِينَ أَلْسِنَتُهُمْ رَطْبَةٌ بِذِكْرِ اللهِ عَزَّ وَجَلَّ يَدْخُلُ أَحَدُهُمُ الْجَنَّةَ وَهُوَ يَضْحَكُ

"Verily, one who keeps his tongue moist with the remembrance of Allah the Almighty, will enter *Jannah* laughing." (*Ḥilyat al-Awliyāʾ* 1/219)

f. *The Prophet's (ﷺ) astonishing dream of the Hereafter*

ʿAbd al-Raḥmān ibn Samurah (ﷺ) reported: The Messenger of Allah (ﷺ) came out to us and said:

إِنِّي رَأَيْتُ الْبَارِحَةَ عَجَبًا رَأَيْتُ رَجُلًا مِنْ أُمَّتِي قَدِ احْتَوَشَتْهُ مَلَائِكَةٌ فَجَاءَهُ وُضُوؤُهُ فَاسْتَنْقَذَهُ مِنْ ذَلِكَ وَرَأَيْتُ رَجُلًا مِنْ أُمَّتِي قَدِ احْتَوَشَتْهُ الشَّيَاطِينُ فَجَاءَهُ ذِكْرُ اللَّهِ فَخَلَّصَهُ مِنْهُمْ وَرَأَيْتُ رَجُلًا مِنْ أُمَّتِي يَلْهَثُ عَطَشًا مِنَ الْعَطَشِ فَجَاءَهُ صِيَامُ رَمَضَانَ فَسَقَاهُ وَرَأَيْتُ رَجُلًا مِنْ أُمَّتِي بَيْنَ يَدَيْهِ ظُلْمَةٌ وَمِنْ خَلْفِهِ ظُلْمَةٌ وَعَنْ يَمِينِهِ ظُلْمَةٌ وَعَنْ شِمَالِهِ ظُلْمَةٌ وَمِنْ فَوْقِهِ ظُلْمَةٌ وَمِنْ تَحْتِهِ ظُلْمَةٌ فَجَاءَهُ حَجُّهُ وَعُمْرَتُهُ فَاسْتَخْرَجَاهُ مِنَ الظُّلْمَةِ وَرَأَيْتُ رَجُلًا مِنْ أُمَّتِي جَاءَهُ مَلَكُ الْمَوْتِ يَقْبِضُ رُوحَهُ فَجَاءَهُ بِرُّهُ بِوَالِدَيْهِ فَرَدَّهُ عَنْهُ وَرَأَيْتُ رَجُلًا مِنْ أُمَّتِي يُكَلِّمُ الْمُؤْمِنِينَ وَلَا

يُكَلِّمُوهُ فَجَاءَتْهُ صِلَةُ الرَّحِمِ فَقَالَتْ إِنَّ هَذَا وَاصِلٌ كَانَ وَاصِلًا لِرَحِمِهِ فَكَلَّمَهُمْ وَكَلَّمُوهُ وَصَارَ مَعَهُمْ وَرَأَيْتُ رَجُلًا مِنْ أُمَّتِي يَأْتِي النَّاسَ وَهُمْ حِلَقٌ فَكُلَّمَا أَتَى عَلَى حَلْقَةٍ طُرِدَ فَجَاءَهُ اغْتِسَالُهُ مِنَ الْجَنَابَةِ فَأَخَذَهُ بِيَدِهِ فَأَجْلَسَهُ مَعَهُمْ وَرَأَيْتُ رَجُلًا مِنْ أُمَّتِي يَتَّقِي وَهَجَ النَّارِ بِيَدَيْهِ عَنْ وَجْهِهِ فَجَاءَتْهُ صَدَقَتُهُ وَصَارَتْ ظِلًّا عَلَى رَأْسِهِ وَسِتْرًا عَلَى وَجْهِهِ وَرَأَيْتُ رَجُلًا مِنْ أُمَّتِي جَاءَتْهُ زَبَانِيَةُ الْعَذَابِ فَجَاءَهُ أَمْرُهُ بِالْمَعْرُوفِ وَنَهْيُهُ عَنِ الْمُنْكَرِ فَاسْتَنْقَذَهُ مِنْ ذَلِكَ وَرَأَيْتُ رَجُلًا مِنْ أُمَّتِي هَوَى فِي النَّارِ فَجَاءَتْهُ دُمُوعُهُ الَّتِي بَكَى مِنْ خَشْيَةِ اللَّهِ فَأَخْرَجَتْهُ مِنَ النَّارِ وَرَأَيْتُ رَجُلًا مِنْ أُمَّتِي قَدْ هَوَتْ صَحِيفَتُهُ إِلَى شِمَالِهِ فَجَاءَهُ خَوْفُهُ مِنَ اللَّهِ فَأَخَذَ صَحِيفَتَهُ فَجَعَلَهَا فِي يَمِينِهِ وَرَأَيْتُ رَجُلًا مِنْ أُمَّتِي يَرْعَدُ كَمَا تَرْعَدُ السَّعَفَةُ فَجَاءَهُ حُسْنُ ظَنِّهِ بِاللَّهِ فَسَكَّنَ رِعْدَتَهُ وَرَأَيْتُ رَجُلًا مِنْ أُمَّتِي يَزْحَفُ عَلَى الصِّرَاطِ مَرَّةً وَيَحْبُو مَرَّةً وَيَتَعَلَّقُ مَرَّةً فَجَاءَتْهُ صَلَاتُهُ عَلَيَّ فَأَخَذَتْ بِيَدِهِ فَأَقَامَتْهُ عَلَى الصِّرَاطِ حَتَّى جَاوَزَ وَرَأَيْتُ رَجُلًا مِنْ أُمَّتِي انْتَهَى إِلَى أَبْوَابِ الْجَنَّةِ فَغُلِّقَتِ الْأَبْوَابُ دُونَهُ فَجَاءَتْهُ شَهَادَةُ أَنْ لَا إِلَهَ إِلَّا اللَّهُ فَأَخَذَتْهُ بِيَدِهِ فَأَدْخَلَتْهُ الْجَنَّةَ

"Verily, I saw something wondrous last night. I saw a man of my nation as angels were holding him back, and his ablution came to save him from that. I saw a man of my nation surrounded by devils, and the remembrance of Allah came to free him from them. I saw a man of my nation suffering from extreme thirst, and his fasting in *Ramaḍān* came to give him drink. I saw a man of my nation with darkness before him, darkness behind him, darkness to his right, darkness to his left, darkness above him, and darkness below him, and his pilgrimages came to bring him out of darkness. I saw a man of my nation to whom the angel of death came to take his soul, and his righteousness to his parents came and turned the angel back. I saw a man of my nation to whom the believers would not speak, and his maintenance of family ties came and it said: 'Verily, he is one who has maintained family ties, so speak to him,' and he became one of them. I saw a man of my nation come to people sitting in circles and every circle he came to drove him away, and his ritual bath from major impurity led him by the hand and seated him next to them. I saw a man of my nation shielding his face from the heat of *Jahannam*, and his charity came to give him shade and cover his face. I saw a man of my nation to whom the angels of punishment came, and his enjoining good and forbidding evil came to save him from that. I saw a man of my nation falling into *Jahannam*, and the tears which he shed for reverence of Allah came to pull him out of the Fire. I saw a man of my nation whose scroll fell into his left hand, and his fear of Allah came to place his scroll in his right hand. I saw a man of my nation swaying in the wind like a palm tree, and his good thoughts of Allah came to calm his shaking. I saw a man of my nation crawling across the bridge over *Jahannam*, at times kneeling, at times clinging to it, and his blessings over me came to take him by the hand and stand him up upon the bridge until he passed over it. I saw a man of my nation who was stopped at the Gates of *Jannah* and every gate was locked for him, and his testimony that 'there is no god but Allah' came to take him by the hand and lead him into *Jannah*." (*al-Muʿjam al-Kabīr* 39, *Ṣaḥīḥ li-ghayrihī* (authentic due to external evidences), according to Ibn Taymiyyah)

g. *The people of Jannah's only regret is not remembering Allah more*

Muʿādh ibn Jabal (ﷺ) reported: The Messenger of Allah (ﷺ) said:

لَيْسَ يَتَحَسَّرُ أَهْلُ الْجَنَّةِ إِلَّا عَلَى سَاعَةٍ مَرَّتْ بِهِمْ لَمْ يَذْكُرُوا اللهَ فِيهَا

"The people of *Jannah* will have no regrets, except for moments that passed by them in which they did not remember Allah." (*al-Muʿjam al-Kabīr* 182, *Ḥasan* according to al-Suyūṭī)

Abū Hurayrah (ﷺ) reported: The Messenger of Allah (ﷺ) said:

مَا قَعَدَ قَوْمٌ مَقْعَدًا لَا يَذْكُرُونَ فِيهِ اللهَ عَزَّ وَجَلَّ وَيُصَلُّونَ عَلَى النَّبِيِّ صَلَّى اللهُ عَلَيْهِ وَسَلَّمَ إِلَّا كَانَ عَلَيْهِمْ حَسْرَةً يَوْمَ الْقِيَامَةِ وَإِنْ دَخَلُوا الْجَنَّةَ لِلثَّوَابِ

"No people sit in a gathering in which they did not remember Allah, nor send blessings upon the Prophet (ﷺ), but that it will cause them grief on the Day of Resurrection, even if they are rewarded with entry into *Jannah*." (*Musnad Aḥmad* 9965, *Ṣaḥīḥ* according to al-Arnāʾūṭ)

h. Those mentioning Allah remembered by the Throne

Al-Nuʿmān ibn Bashīr (ﷺ) reported: The Messenger of Allah (ﷺ) said:

إِنَّ مِمَّا تَذْكُرُونَ مِنْ جَلَالِ اللَّهِ التَّسْبِيحَ وَالتَّهْلِيلَ وَالتَّحْمِيدَ يَنْعَطِفْنَ حَوْلَ الْعَرْشِ لَهُنَّ دَوِيٌّ كَدَوِيِّ النَّحْلِ تُذَكِّرُ بِصَاحِبِهَا أَمَا يُحِبُّ أَحَدُكُمْ أَنْ يَكُونَ لَهُ أَوْ لَا يَزَالَ لَهُ مَنْ يُذَكِّرُ بِهِ

"Verily, among what you mention of the majesty of Allah, His glorification, declaration of His oneness, and His praise, circles around the Throne, buzzing like bees in reminder of who said them. Would one of you not like to be continuously remembered in this way?" (*Sunan Ibn Mājah* 3809, *Ṣaḥīḥ* according to al-Albānī)

i. One of the best deeds is to die while making dhikr

Muʿādh ibn Jabal (ﷺ) reported that:

I asked the Messenger of Allah (ﷺ): "Which deeds are most beloved to Allah?" The Prophet (ﷺ) said:

أَنْ تَمُوتَ وَلِسَانُكَ رَطْبٌ مِنْ ذِكْرِ اللَّهِ

"That you die while your tongue is moist with the remembrance of Allah." (*Ṣaḥīḥ Ibn Ḥibbān* 818, *Ḥasan* according to Ibn Ḥajar)

j. ***Remove from Jahannam all who remembered Allah***

Anas ibn Mālik (ﷺ) reported: The Prophet (ﷺ) said:

يَقُولُ اللَّهُ أَخْرِجُوا مِنْ النَّارِ مَنْ ذَكَرَنِي يَوْمًا أَوْ خَافَنِي فِي مَقَامٍ

"Allah will say: 'Take out from *Jahannam* whoever remembered me for a day, or who feared to stand before me.'" (*Sunan al-Tirmidhī* 2594, *Ḥasan* according to Ibn Ḥajar)

k. ***Gardens of Jannah***

Anas ibn Mālik (ﷺ) reported: The Messenger of Allah (ﷺ) said:

إِذَا مَرَرْتُمْ بِرِيَاضِ الْجَنَّةِ فَارْتَعُوا

"When you pass by the Gardens of *Jannah*, graze as you like."

They said: "What are the Gardens of *Jannah*?" The Prophet said:

حِلَقُ الذِّكْرِ

"Circles of remembrance." (*Sunan al-Tirmidhī* 3510)

l. ***Ninety-nine Names of Allah will give you Jannah***

Abū Hurayrah (ﷺ) reported: The Messenger of Allah (ﷺ) said:

لِلَّهِ تِسْعَةٌ وَتِسْعُونَ اسْمًا مَنْ حَفِظَهَا دَخَلَ الْجَنَّةَ

"Allah has ninety-nine names. Whoever preserves (memorises) them will enter *Jannah*." (*Ṣaḥīḥ al-Bukhārī* 7392, *Ṣaḥīḥ Muslim* 2677)

m. ***The Soil of Jannah is planted with the Dhikr of Allah***

Ibn Masʿūd (ﷺ) reported that the Prophet (ﷺ) said:

لَقِيتُ إِبْرَاهِيمَ لَيْلَةَ أُسْرِيَ بِي فَقَالَ يَا مُحَمَّدُ أَقْرِئْ أُمَّتَكَ مِنِّي السَّلَامَ وَأَخْبِرْهُمْ أَنَّ الْجَنَّةَ

طَيِّبَةُ التُّرْبَةِ عَذْبَةُ الْمَاءِ وَأَنَّهَا قِيعَانٌ وَأَنَّ غِرَاسَهَا سُبْحَانَ اللَّهِ وَالْحَمْدُ لِلَّهِ وَلَا إِلَهَ إِلَّا اللَّهُ وَاللَّهُ أَكْبَرُ

"I met Ibrāhīm (ﷺ) on the Night of Ascension and he said to me: 'O Muhammad, convey my greetings to your nation, and tell them that *Jannah* has pure soil and sweet water. It is a vast plain land and its seedlings are: 'Glory be to Allah' (*subḥān Allāh*); 'Praise be to Allah' (*al-ḥamdu lillāh*); 'There is no god but Allah' (*lā ilāha illā Allāh*); and 'Allah is Greatest' (*Allāhu Akbar*).

n. ***Saying Lā Ḥawla wa-lā Quwwata illā Billāh***

Qays ibn Saʿd ibn ʿUbādah (رضي الله عنه) narrated that his father offered him to the Prophet (ﷺ) to serve him. He said:

"So the Prophet (ﷺ) passed by me, and I had just performed *Ṣalāh*, so he poked me with his foot and said:

أَلاَ أَدُلُّكَ عَلَى بَابٍ مِنْ أَبْوَابِ الْجَنَّةِ

'Should I not direct you to a gate from the Gates of *Jannah*?' I said: 'Of course.' He (ﷺ) said:

لاَ حَوْلَ وَلاَ قُوَّةَ إِلاَّ بِاللَّهِ

'There is no might nor power except through Allah (*Lā ḥawla wa-lā quwwata illā billāh*).' " (*Sunan al-Tirmidhī* 3581, *Ḥasan Ṣaḥīḥ*)

Muʿādh ibn Jabal (رضي الله عنه) narrates: The Prophet (ﷺ) asked:

أَلاَ أَدُلُّكَ عَلَى بَابٍ مِنْ أَبْوَابِ الْجَنَّةِ

"Should I not inform you of a gate from the Gates of *Jannah*?" I said:

"Of course." He (ﷺ) said:

لاَ حَوْلَ وَلاَ قُوَّةَ إِلاَّ بِاللَّهِ

"There is no might nor power except through Allah (*Lā ḥawla wa-lā quwwata illā billāh*)." (*Musnad Aḥmad* 22115, *Ṣaḥīḥ li-ghayrihi* (authentic due to external evidences), according to al-Albānī)

o. Recitation of this duʿā will make the Prophet (ﷺ) take you by the hand into Jannah

Al-Munaydhir (رضي الله عنه) reported: The Messenger of Allah (ﷺ) said:

مَنْ قَالَ إِذَا أَصْبَحَ رَضِيتُ بِاللهِ رَبًّا وَبِالْإِسْلَامِ دِينًا وَبِمُحَمَّدٍ نَبِيًّا فَأَنَا الزَّعِيمُ لَآخُذَ بِيَدِهِ حَتَّى أُدْخِلَهُ الْجَنَّةَ

"Whoever says when he awakens in the morning: 'I am pleased with Allah as a Lord, with *Islām* as a religion, and with Muhammad as a prophet,' then I am responsible for him and I will surely take him by the hand until he enters *Jannah*." (*al-Muʿjam al-Kabīr lil-Ṭabarānī* 20/355, *Ṣaḥīḥ* according to al-Albānī)

Abū Saʿīd al-Khudrī (رضي الله عنه) reported: The Messenger of Allah (ﷺ) said:

مَنْ رَضِيَ بِاللَّهِ رَبًّا وَبِالْإِسْلَامِ دِينًا وَبِمُحَمَّدٍ نَبِيًّا وَجَبَتْ لَهُ الْجَنَّةُ

"Whoever is pleased with Allah as a Lord, with *Islām* as a religion, and with Muhammad as a prophet, he must enter *Jannah*." (*Ṣaḥīḥ Muslim* 1884)

p. Reading Sūrah al-Ikhlāṣ enters one into Jannah

Abū Hurayrah (رضي الله عنه) reported: The Prophet (ﷺ) said:

مَنْ قَرَأَ قُلْ هُوَ اللَّهُ أَحَدٌ عَشْرَ مَرَّاتٍ بُنِيَ لَهُ قَصْرٌ فِي الْجَنَّةِ وَمَنْ قَرَأَهَا عِشْرِينَ مَرَّةً بُنِيَ لَهُ قَصْرَانِ وَمَنْ قَرَأَهَا ثَلَاثِينَ مَرَّةً بُنِيَ لَهُ ثَلَاثٌ

"Whoever recites ten times: 'Say: He is Allah–One,' (al-Ikhlāṣ, 112), a palace will be built for him in *Jannah*. Whoever recites it twenty times, two palaces will be built for him. Whoever recites it thirty times, three palaces will be built for him." (*al-Muʿjam al-Awsaṭ lil-Ṭabarānī 281, Ṣaḥīḥ* according to al-Albānī)

Muʿādh ibn Anas (🙂) reported: The Prophet (🙂) said:

مَنْ قَرَأَ قُلْ هُوَ اللَّهُ أَحَدٌ حَتَّى يَخْتِمَهَا عَشْرَ مَرَّاتٍ بَنَى اللَّهُ لَهُ قَصْرًا فِي الْجَنَّةِ

"Whoever recites the entire chapter - 'Say: He is Allah—One' (*al-Ikhlāṣ*, 112) - ten times, Allah will build a palace for him in *Jannah*." (*Musnad Aḥmad 15610, Ṣaḥīḥ* according to al-Albānī)

Abū Hurayrah (🙂) reported:

I met with the Prophet (🙂) and he heard a man reciting the verses:

قُلْ هُوَ اللَّهُ أَحَدٌ اللَّهُ الصَّمَدُ

"Say: He is Allah—One, the Eternal Refuge" (*al-Ikhlāṣ*, 112:1-2).

The Prophet (🙂) said:

وَجَبَتْ

"It is *wājib* [for him]." I said, "What is *wājib* [for him]?" The Prophet (🙂) said:

الْجَنَّةُ

"*Jannah*." (*Sunan al-Tirmidhī* 2897, *Ṣaḥīḥ* according to al-Albānī)

Anas ibn Mālik (ﷺ) reported:

A man said: "O Messenger of Allah, I love this chapter:

قُلْ هُوَ اللَّهُ أَحَدٌ

'Say: He is Allah—One.' " (*al-Ikhlāṣ*, 112:1)

The Messenger of Allah (ﷺ) said:

حُبُّكَ إِيَّاهَا أَدْخَلَكَ الْجَنَّةَ

"Your love for it will admit you into *Jannah*." (*Ṣaḥīḥ al-Bukhārī* 742)

q. *Saying 'subḥān Allāh', 'al-ḥamdu lillāh' and 'Allāhu Akbar' enters one into Jannah*

ʿAbdullāh ibn ʿAmr (ﷺ) reported: The Messenger of Allah (ﷺ) said:

خَلَّتَانِ لَا يُحْصِيهِمَا رَجُلٌ مُسْلِمٌ إِلَّا دَخَلَ الْجَنَّةَ أَلَا وَهُمَا يَسِيرٌ وَمَنْ يَعْمَلُ بِهِمَا قَلِيلٌ يُسَبِّحُ اللهَ فِي دُبُرِ كُلِّ صَلَاةٍ عَشْرًا وَيَحْمَدُهُ عَشْرًا وَيُكَبِّرُهُ عَشْرًا فَتِلْكَ خَمْسُونَ وَمِائَةٌ بِاللِّسَانِ وَأَلْفٌ وَخَمْسُ مِائَةٍ فِي الْمِيزَانِ وَإِذَا أَخَذْتَ مَضْجَعَكَ تُسَبِّحُهُ وَتُكَبِّرُهُ وَتَحْمَدُهُ مِائَةً فَتِلْكَ مِائَةٌ بِاللِّسَانِ وَأَلْفٌ فِي الْمِيزَانِ فَأَيُّكُمْ يَعْمَلُ فِي الْيَوْمِ وَاللَّيْلَةِ أَلْفَيْ وَخَمْسَ مِائَةِ سَيِّئَةٍ قَالُوا فَكَيْفَ لَا نُحْصِيهَا قَالَ يَأْتِي أَحَدَكُمُ الشَّيْطَانُ وَهُوَ فِي صَلَاتِهِ فَيَقُولُ اذْكُرْ كَذَا اذْكُرْ كَذَا حَتَّى يَنْفَتِلَ فَلَعَلَّهُ أَنْ لَا يَفْعَلَ وَيَأْتِيهِ وَهُوَ فِي مَضْجَعِهِ فَلَا يَزَالُ يُنَوِّمُهُ حَتَّى يَنَامَ

"There are two practices no *muslim* man preserves but that he will enter *Jannah*. Surely, they are both easy yet few act upon them. Glorify Allah at the end of every prayer ten times, praise Him ten times, and exalt Him ten times. These are one hundred and fifty upon the tongue, but one thousand and five hundred upon the Scale. When you retire to your bed, glorify Him, exalt Him, and praise Him one hundred times. These are one hundred upon the tongue, but one thousand upon the Scale. Which one of you would commit two thousand and five hundred sins in a day and night?" They said: "How could we not preserve them?" The Prophet (ﷺ) said, "*Shayṭān* comes to one of you while he is praying and he whispers for him to remember this and that until he turns away and, perhaps, he does not do it. While in his bed, *Shayṭān* continues to lure him to sleep until he falls asleep." (*Sunan al-Tirmidhī* 3410, *Ṣaḥīḥ*)

Ibn ʿAbbās (رضي الله عنه) reported: The Prophet (ﷺ) said:

أَوَّلُ مَنْ يُدْعَى إِلَى الْجَنَّةِ الْحَمَّادُونَ الَّذِينَ يَحْمَدُونَ اللَّهَ عَلَى السَّرَّاءِ وَالضَّرَّاءِ

"The first to be called to *Jannah* are those who always praised Allah in times of prosperity and adversity." (*al-Muʿjam al-Kabīr lil-Ṭabarānī* 12345, *Ṣaḥīḥ* according to al-Suyūṭī)

r. A memoriser of the Qur'an will ascend the Levels of Jannah

Abū Saʿīd al-Khudrī (رضي الله عنه) reported: The Messenger of Allah (ﷺ) said:

يُقَالُ لِصَاحِبِ الْقُرْآنِ إِذَا دَخَلَ الْجَنَّةَ اقْرَأْ وَاصْعَدْ فَيَقْرَأُ وَيَصْعَدُ بِكُلِّ آيَةٍ دَرَجَةً حَتَّى يَقْرَأَ آخِرَ شَيْءٍ مَعَهُ

"It will be said to the companion of the Qur'an when he enters *Jannah*: 'Recite and ascend!' Thus, he will recite and ascend one level for each verse until he recites the last one with him." (*Sunan Ibn Mājah* 3780, *Ṣaḥīḥ* according to al-Albānī)

Jābir (ﷺ) reported: The Prophet (ﷺ) said:

الْقُرْآنُ مُشَفَّعٌ وَمَاحِلٌ مُصَدَّقٌ مَنْ جَعَلَهُ إِمَامَهُ قَادَهُ إِلَى الْجَنَّةِ وَمَنْ جَعَلَهُ خَلْفَ ظَهْرِهِ سَاقَهُ إِلَى النَّارِ

"The Qur'an is an intercessor and a truthful prosecutor. Whoever puts it in front of himself, it will lead him to *Jannah*. Whoever throws it behind his back, it will drive him into *Jahannam*." (*Ṣaḥīḥ Ibn Ḥibbān* 124, *Jayyid* (good) according to al-Arnāʾūṭ)

s. *Asking Allah for Jannah seven times in a day*

Abū Hurayrah (ﷺ) reported: The Messenger of Allah (ﷺ) said:

مَا اسْتَجَارَ عَبْدٌ مِنَ النَّارِ سَبْعَ مَرَّاتٍ فِي يَوْمٍ إِلَّا قَالَتِ النَّارُ يَا رَبِّ إِنَّ عَبْدَكَ فُلَانًا قَدِ اسْتَجَارَكَ مِنِّي فَأَجِرْهُ وَلَا يَسْأَلُ اللَّهَ عَبْدٌ الْجَنَّةَ فِي يَوْمٍ سَبْعَ مَرَّاتٍ إِلَّا قَالَتِ الْجَنَّةُ يَا رَبِّ إِنَّ عَبْدَكَ فُلَانًا سَأَلَنِي فَأَدْخِلْهُ

"No servant seeks protection from *Jahannam* seven times in a day but that *Jahannam* says: 'O Lord, Your servant has sought Your protection from me, so protect him!' No servant asks Allah for *Jannah* seven times in a day but that *Jannah* says: 'O Lord, Your servant has asked for me, so admit him!' " (*Musnad Abī Yaʿlā* 6192, *Ṣaḥīḥ* according to al-Albānī)

Anas ibn Mālik (ﷺ) reported: The Messenger of Allah (ﷺ) said:

مَنْ سَأَلَ اللَّهَ الْجَنَّةَ ثَلَاثَ مَرَّاتٍ قَالَتْ الْجَنَّةُ اللَّهُمَّ أَدْخِلْهُ الْجَنَّةَ وَمَنْ اسْتَجَارَ مِنْ النَّارِ ثَلَاثَ مَرَّاتٍ قَالَتْ النَّارُ اللَّهُمَّ أَجِرْهُ مِنْ النَّارِ

"Whoever asks Allah for *Jannah* three times, *Jannah* will say: 'O Allah, admit him into *Jannah*!' Whoever seeks protection from *Jahannam* three times, *Jahannam* will say: 'O Allah, save him from *Jahannam*!' "

(*Sunan al-Tirmidhī* 2572, *Ṣaḥīḥ* according to al-Albānī)

t. ***Sitting near the imam on Friday***

Samurah ibn Jundub (ﷺ) reported: The Messenger of Allah (ﷺ) said:

احْضُرُوا الذِّكْرَ وَادْنُوا مِنَ الْإِمَامِ فَإِنَّ الرَّجُلَ لَا يَزَالُ يَتَبَاعَدُ حَتَّى يُؤَخَّرَ فِي الْجَنَّةِ وَإِنْ دَخَلَهَا

"Be present at the sermon and come close to the imam. Verily, a man continues to distance himself until he is delayed from *Jannah*, even though he will eventually enter it." (*Sunan Abī Dāwūd* 1108, *Ṣaḥīḥ* according to al-Arnāʾūṭ)

u. ***Sending Salutations upon the Prophet (ﷺ)***

Abū Ṭalḥah (ﷺ) reported: The Messenger of Allah (ﷺ) said:

أَتَانِي آتٍ مِنْ رَبِّي عَزَّ وَجَلَّ فَقَالَ مَنْ صَلَّى عَلَيْكَ مِنْ أُمَّتِكَ صَلَاةً كَتَبَ اللهُ لَهُ بِهَا عَشْرَ حَسَنَاتٍ وَمَحَا عَنْهُ عَشْرَ سَيِّئَاتٍ وَرَفَعَ لَهُ عَشْرَ دَرَجَاتٍ وَرَدَّ عَلَيْهِ مِثْلَهَا

"A visitor came to me from my Lord the Almighty and he said: 'Whoever among your nation blesses you, Allah will record for him ten good deeds, He will erase ten bad deeds, He will raise him ten degrees, and the angel will respond with the same.' " (*Musnad Aḥmad* 16352, *Ṣaḥīḥ* according to al-Albānī)

Ibn ʿAbbās (ﷺ) reported: The Messenger of Allah (ﷺ) said:

مَنْ نَسِيَ الصَّلَاةَ عَلَيَّ خَطِئَ طَرِيقَ الْجَنَّةِ

"Whoever forgets to send blessings upon me has missed a path to *Jannah*." (*Sunan Ibn Mājah* 908, *Ṣaḥīḥ* according to al-Albānī)

Ibn Masʿūd (؇) reported: The Messenger of Allah (؇) said:

أَوْلَى النَّاسِ بِي يَوْمَ الْقِيَامَةِ أَكْثَرُهُمْ عَلَيَّ صَلَاةً

"The closest of people to me on the Day of Resurrection are those who sent the most blessings upon me." (*Sunan al-Tirmidhī* 484, Ḥasan according to al-Tirmidhī)

Bāb al-Dhikr, where souls find their delight,
On Judgment Day, they shine in Allah's sight.

The reward of *dhikr*, a treasure so vast,
In *Jannah*'s embrace, they're forever steadfast.

Replying to the *adhān*, a blessed decree,
Leads to *Jannah*'s shade, in happiness and glee.

Planting your trees in *Jannah*'s sacred ground,
With *dhikr*, the seeds of Paradise are found.

Those who remember Allah, their hearts are bright,
In *Jannah*'s gardens, they find pure delight.

The Prophet's dream of the Hereafter, so sublime,
A vision of *Jannah*, a glimpse of eternal prime.

Their only regret: not paying *dhikr* more heed,
In *Jannah*'s bliss, their souls will ever feed.

Those who mention Allah, by the Throne are known,
In Paradise's gardens, they've truly grown.

The best deed, to die in *dhikr*'s embrace,
In *Jannah*'s beauty, they'll find their place.

Remove from Hell those who Allah's name adore,
Through *dhikr*'s blessings, they shall suffer no more.

Gardens of *Jannah*, where believers tread,
In *dhikr*'s fragrance, their souls are led.

The 99 Names of Allah, a path to *Jannah*'s gate,
In *dhikr*'s garden, their hearts resonate.

The soil of *Jannah*, with *dhikr*'s essence sown,
In Paradise's embrace, they find their own.

Saying "*lā ḥawla wa lā quwwata illā billāh*" with might,
Into *Jannah*'s glory, they enter the light.

Reciting the *duʿā* that contents the humble's soul,
By the Prophet's hand they will surely reach their goal.

Sūrat al-Ikhlāṣ, a key to heaven's door,
In *Jannah*'s realms, they'll forever soar.

"*Subḥān Allah, al-ḥamdu lillāh, Allāhu Akbar*" they said,
Such heavy words, to *Jannah* they surely led.

A memoriser of the Qur'an, ascending high,
In *Jannah*'s levels, they reach the sky.

Seven times a day, for *Jannah* they plea,
In the Gardens of Paradise, their soul will forever be.

Sitting near the imam on Friday's light,
In *Jannah*'s blessings, their hearts ignite.

Sending salutations upon the Prophet's name,
The blessings of *Jannah*, they'll forever claim.

لله بابا في الجنة لا يدخله إلا من
عفا عن مظلمة

CHAPTER

Eight

BĀB AL-KĀẒIMĪN AL-GHAYẒ WA-L-ʿĀFĪN ʿAN AL-NĀS

GATE OF SUPPRESSING ONE'S ANGER AND FORGIVING THE PEOPLE[4]

4 According to al-Ḥasan al-Baṣrī, Imam al-Nawawī, and Ibn Ḥajar (ﷺ).

This door is reserved for those who suppress their anger and pardon others. It is based upon a *Mursal Ḥadīth* narrated by al-Ḥasan al-Baṣrī (ﷺ):

إن لله بابًا في الْجنَّة لَا يدْخلهُ إلاَّ من عَفا عَن مظْلمَة

"There is a gate in *Jannah* that none will enter by except the one who forgives others' injustice." (Reported by Aḥmad as quoted by Ibn Ḥajar in *al-Fatḥ al-Bāri* 7/28)

ٱلَّذِينَ يُنفِقُونَ فِى ٱلسَّرَّآءِ وَٱلضَّرَّآءِ وَٱلْكَـٰظِمِينَ ٱلْغَيْظَ وَٱلْعَافِينَ عَنِ ٱلنَّاسِ ۗ وَٱللَّهُ يُحِبُّ ٱلْمُحْسِنِينَ ﴿١٣٤﴾

"Who spend [in the cause of Allah] during ease and hardship and who restrain anger and who pardon the people - and Allah loves the doers of good." (*Āl ʿImrān*, 3:134)

إِن تُبْدُوا۟ خَيْرًا أَوْ تُخْفُوهُ أَوْ تَعْفُوا۟ عَن سُوٓءٍ فَإِنَّ ٱللَّهَ كَانَ عَفُوًّا قَدِيرًا ﴿١٤٩﴾

"If [instead] you show [some] good or conceal it or pardon an offense - indeed, Allah is ever Pardoning and Competent." (*al-Nisāʾ*, 4:149)

وَإِنْ عَاقَبْتُمْ فَعَاقِبُوا۟ بِمِثْلِ مَا عُوقِبْتُم بِهِۦ ۖ وَلَئِن صَبَرْتُمْ لَهُوَ خَيْرٌ لِّلصَّـٰبِرِينَ ﴿١٢٦﴾

"And if you punish [an enemy, O believers], punish with an equivalent of that with which you were harmed. But if you are patient - it is better for those who are patient." (*al-Naḥl*, 16:126)

وَلَمَن صَبَرَ وَغَفَرَ إِنَّ ذَٰلِكَ لَمِنْ عَزْمِ ٱلْأُمُورِ ﴿٤٣﴾

"And whoever is patient and forgives - indeed, that is of the matters [requiring] determination." (*al-Shūra*, 42:43)

يَـٰٓأَيُّهَا ٱلَّذِينَ ءَامَنُوٓا۟ إِنَّ مِنْ أَزْوَٰجِكُمْ وَأَوْلَـٰدِكُمْ عَدُوًّا لَّكُمْ فَٱحْذَرُوهُمْ ۚ وَإِن تَعْفُوا۟ وَتَصْفَحُوا۟ وَتَغْفِرُوا۟ فَإِنَّ ٱللَّهَ غَفُورٌ رَّحِيمٌ ﴿١٤﴾

"But if you pardon and overlook and forgive - then indeed, Allah is Forgiving and Merciful." (al-Taghābun, 64:14)

a. *Allah has mercy on a man who forgives debts*

Ḥudhayfah (☺) reported: The Messenger of Allah (☺) said:

تَلَقَّتُ الْمَلَائِكَةُ رُوحَ رَجُلٍ مِمَّنْ كَانَ قَبْلَكُمْ فَقَالُوا أَعَمِلْتَ مِنَ الْخَيْرِ شَيْئًا قَالَ لَا قَالُوا تَذَكَّرْ قَالَ كُنْتُ أُدَايِنُ النَّاسَ فَآمُرُ فِتْيَانِي أَنْ يُنْظِرُوا الْمُعْسِرَ وَيَتَجَوَّزُوا عَنِ الْمُوسِرِ قَالَ قَالَ اللَّهُ عَزَّ وَجَلَّ تَجَوَّزُوا عَنْهُ

"The angels received the soul of a man who lived before you. They said: 'Have you done anything good?' The man said: 'No.' They said: 'Try to remember.' The man said: 'I used to give loans and I would order my servants to give respite to those in difficulty, and to overlook the faults of those in ease.' Allah the Almighty said: 'Overlook his faults.'" (Ṣaḥīḥ al-Bukhārī 1971, Ṣaḥīḥ Muslim 1560)

Abū Hurayrah (☺) reported: The Messenger of Allah (☺) said:

كَانَ الرَّجُلُ يُدَايِنُ النَّاسَ فَكَانَ يَقُولُ لِفَتَاهُ إِذَا أَتَيْتَ مُعْسِرًا فَتَجَاوَزْ عَنْهُ لَعَلَّ اللَّهَ أَنْ يَتَجَاوَزَ عَنَّا قَالَ فَلَقِيَ اللَّهَ فَتَجَاوَزَ عَنْهُ

"A man would give loans to the people and he would say to his servant: 'If the debtor is in hardship you should forgive the debt that perhaps Allah will relieve us.' So, when he met Allah, He relieved him. (Ṣaḥīḥ al-Bukhārī 3293, Ṣaḥīḥ Muslim 1562)

ʿUthmān ibn ʿAffān (☺) reported: The Messenger of Allah (☺) said:

أَدْخَلَ اللَّهُ عَزَّ وَجَلَّ رَجُلًا كَانَ سَهْلًا مُشْتَرِيًا وَبَائِعًا وَقَاضِيًا وَمُقْتَضِيًا الْجَنَّةَ

"Allah the Almighty will admit a man into *Jannah* who was easy in his buying and selling, in his paying debts and seeking repayments." (*Sunan al-Nasāʾī* 4696, *Ṣaḥīḥ* according to Aḥmad Shākir)

b. ***Forgive others and Allah will forgive you***

ʿAbdullāh ibn ʿAmr (رضي الله عنه) reported: The Prophet (ﷺ) said:

ارْحَمُوا تُرْحَمُوا وَاغْفِرُوا يَغْفِرْ اللَّهُ لَكُمْ

"Be merciful to others and you will receive mercy. Forgive others and Allah will forgive you." (*Musnad Aḥmad* 6541, *Ṣaḥīḥ* according to Aḥmad Shākir)

c. ***Allah raises the one who forgives others***

Abū Hurayrah (رضي الله عنه) narrates that the Messenger of Allah (ﷺ) said:

مَا نَقَصَتْ صَدَقَةٌ مِنْ مَالٍ وَمَا زَادَ اللَّهُ عَبْدًا بِعَفْوٍ إِلاَّ عِزًّا وَمَا تَوَاضَعَ أَحَدٌ لِلَّهِ إِلاَّ رَفَعَهُ اللَّهُ

"Charity does not decrease wealth. No one pardons except that Allah increases him in honour, and no one humbles himself before Allah except that Allah raises him in status." (*Ṣaḥīḥ Muslim* 2588)

Anas ibn Mālik (رضي الله عنه) reported: The Prophet (ﷺ) said:

إِذَا وَقَفَ الْعِبَادُ لِلْحِسَابِ يُنَادِي مُنَادٍ لِيَقُمْ مَنْ أَجْرُهُ عَلَى اللَّهِ فَلْيَدْخُلِ الْجَنَّةَ ثُمَّ يُنَادِي الثَّانِيَةَ لِيَقُمْ مَنْ أَجْرُهُ عَلَى اللَّهِ فَيُقَالُ وَمَنْ ذَا الَّذِي أَجْرُهُ عَلَى اللَّهِ فَيَقُولُ الْعَافُونَ عَنِ النَّاسِ فَقَامَ كَذَا وَكَذَا فَدَخَلُوهَا بِغَيْرِ حِسَابٍ

"When the worshipers stand to be held to account, a heavenly caller will announce: 'Let them stand to be rewarded by Allah.' Thus, they will enter *Jannah*. A second caller will announce: 'Let them stand to be rewarded by Allah.' It will be said: 'They are those who forgave people.' Thus, so many will stand and enter *Jannah* without account." (*Makārim al-Akhlāq lil-Ṭabarānī* 55, Ḥasan according to al-Mundhirī)

d. Not admitted into Jannah until they reconcile

Abū Hurayrah (﷠) reported: The Messenger of Allah (ﷺ) said:

تُفْتَحُ أَبْوَابُ الْجَنَّةِ يَوْمَ الِاثْنَيْنِ وَيَوْمَ الْخَمِيسِ فَيُغْفَرُ لِكُلِّ عَبْدٍ لَا يُشْرِكُ بِاللَّهِ شَيْئًا إِلَّا رَجُلًا كَانَتْ بَيْنَهُ وَبَيْنَ أَخِيهِ شَحْنَاءُ فَيُقَالُ أَنْظِرُوا هَذَيْنِ حَتَّى يَصْطَلِحَا أَنْظِرُوا هَذَيْنِ حَتَّى يَصْطَلِحَا أَنْظِرُوا هَذَيْنِ حَتَّى يَصْطَلِحَا

"The Gates of *Jannah* are opened on Monday and Thursday. Allah forgives every servant who does not associate anything with him, except a man with enmity between himself and his brother. It will be said: 'Delay these two until they reconcile, delay these two until they reconcile, delay these two until they reconcile.' " (*Ṣaḥīḥ Muslim* 2565)

Ibn ʿAbbās (﷠) reported: The Messenger of Allah (ﷺ) said:

لَا يَحِلُّ الْهَجْرُ فَوْقَ ثَلَاثَةِ أَيَّامٍ فَإِنْ الْتَقَيَا فَسَلَّمَ أَحَدُهُمَا عَلَى الْآخَرِ فَرَدَّ عَلَيْهِ الْآخَرُ السَّلَامَ اشْتَرَكَا فِي الْأَجْرِ وَإِنْ أَبَى الْآخَرُ أَنْ يَرُدَّ السَّلَامَ بَرِئَ هَذَا مِنَ الْإِثْمِ وَبَاءَ بِهِ الْآخَرُ وَقَدْ خَشِيتُ إِنْ مَاتَا وَهُمَا مُتَهَاجِرَانِ أَنْ لَا يَجْتَمِعَا فِي الْجَنَّةِ

"It is not lawful to boycott for more than three days. If the two meet and one greets the other with peace and receives a response, they will share the reward. If the other refuses to return his greeting, he is free of sin and it backfires against the one boycotting. I fear that if the two die while boycotting each other, they will not be together in *Jannah*." (*al-Muʿjam al-Awsaṭ* 8925, Ṣaḥīḥ li-ghayrihī (authentic due to external evidence), according to al-Albānī)

e. *Suppressing anger saves one from Jahannam*

Anas ibn Mālik (ﷺ) reported: The Messenger of Allah (ﷺ) said:

مَنْ خَزَنَ لِسَانَهُ سَتَرَ اللَّهُ عَوْرَتَهُ وَمَنْ كَفَّ غَضَبَهُ كَفَّ اللَّهُ عَنْهُ عَذَابَهُ يَوْمَ الْقِيَامَةِ وَمَنِ اعْتَذَرَ إِلَى اللَّهِ عَزَّ وَجَلَّ قَبِلَ عُذْرَهُ

"Whoever restricts his tongue, Allah will cover his faults. Whoever restrains his anger, Allah will restrain his punishment on the Day of Resurrection. Whoever apologises to Allah, Allah the Almighty will accept his apology." (*Shuʿab al-Īmān* 7818, *Ḥasan* according to al-Albānī)

f. *Most beloved to Allah*

Ibn ʿUmar (ﷺ) reported: The Prophet (ﷺ) said:

أَحَبُّ النَّاسِ إِلَى اللَّهِ أَنْفَعُهُمْ لِلنَّاسِ وَأَحَبُّ الأَعْمَالِ إِلَى اللَّهِ سُرُورٌ تُدْخِلُهُ عَلَى مُسْلِمٍ أَوْ تَكْشِفُ عَنْهُ كُرْبَةً أَوْ تَقْضِي عَنْهُ دِينًا أَوْ تَطْرُدُ عَنْهُ جُوعًا وَلَأَنْ أَمْشِيَ مَعَ أَخٍ لِي فِي حَاجَةٍ أَحَبُّ إِلَيَّ مِنْ أَنْ أَعْتَكِفَ فِي هَذَا الْمَسْجِدِ يَعْنِي مَسْجِدَ الْمَدِينَةِ شَهْرًا وَمَنْ كَفَّ غَضَبَهُ سَتَرَ اللَّهُ عَوْرَتَهُ وَمَنْ كَظَمَ غَيْظَهُ وَلَوْ شَاءَ أَنْ يُمْضِيَهُ أَمْضَاهُ مَلأَ اللَّهُ عَزَّ وَجَلَّ قَلْبَهُ أَمْنًا يَوْمَ الْقِيَامَةِ وَمَنْ مَشَى مَعَ أَخِيهِ فِي حَاجَةٍ حَتَّى أَثْبَتَهَا لَهُ أَثْبَتَ اللَّهُ عَزَّ وَجَلَّ قَدَمَهُ عَلَى الصِّرَاطِ يَوْمَ تَزِلُّ فِيهِ الأَقْدَامُ

"The most beloved people to Allah are those who are most beneficial to people. The most beloved deed to Allah is to make a *muslim* happy, or to remove one of his troubles, or to forgive his debt, or to feed his hunger. That I walk with a brother regarding a need is more beloved to me than that I seclude myself in this *masjid* in *Madīnah* for a month. Whoever swallows his anger, then Allah will conceal his faults. Whoever suppresses his rage, even though he could fulfill his anger if he wished, then Allah will secure his heart on the Day of Resurrection. Whoever walks with his brother regarding a need until he secures it for him, then Allah the Almighty will make his footing firm across the bridge on the day when the footings are shaken." (*al-Muʿjam al-Awsaṭ* 6192, *Ṣaḥīḥ* according to al-Albānī)

g. *Do not get angry and Jannah is yours*

Abū al-Dardāʾ (ﷺ) said: I asked the Messenger of Allah (ﷺ):

"Tell me of a deed which will earn me admission into *Jannah*." He (ﷺ) said:

لا تَغْضَبْ وَلَكَ الْجَنَّةُ

"Do not get angry, and *Jannah* will be yours." (*al-Muʿjam al-Awsaṭ* 2411, *Ṣaḥīḥ* according to al-Albānī, *Ṣaḥīḥ al-Targhīb wa al-Tarhīb* 2749)

h. *Whoever controls his anger is filled with security and faith*

Abū Hurayrah (ﷺ) reported: The Prophet (ﷺ) said:

مَنْ كَظَمَ غَيْظًا وَهُوَ يَقْدِرُعَلَى إِنْفَاذِهِ مَلَأَهُ اللَّهُ أَمْنًا وَإِيمَانًا وقرأ وَالْكَاظِمِينَ الْغَيْظَ وَالْعَافِينَ عَنِ النَّاسِ وَاللَّهُ يُحِبُّ الْمُحْسِنِينَ

"Whoever suppresses his rage while he is capable of unleashing it, then Allah will fill him with assurance and faith." And the Prophet (ﷺ) recited the verse, "They are those who suppress their rage and forgive people, for Allah loves those who do good" (*Āl ʿImrān*, 3:134). (*Tafsīr al-Ṭabarī* 3:134, *Ḥasan* according to al-Suyūṭī and al-Saffārīnī)

i. *He will have any Ḥūr al-ʿAyn in Jannah*

Muʿādh ibn Anas (ﷺ) reported: The Prophet (ﷺ) said:

مَنْ كَظَمَ غَيْظًا - وَهُوَ قَادِرٌ عَلَى أَنْ يُنْفِذَهُ - دَعَاهُ اللَّهُ عَزَّ وَجَلَّ عَلَى رُءُوسِ الْخَلائِقِ يَوْمَ الْقِيَامَةِ حَتَّى يُخَيِّرَهُ اللَّهُ مِنَ الْحُورِ مَا شَاءَ

"Whoever controls his anger at the time when he has the means to act upon it, Allah will call him before all of mankind on the Day of Resurrection and will let him choose of the Ḥūr al-ʿAyn whomever he wants." (*Sunan Abū Dāwūd* 4777, Ḥasan according to al-Albānī in *Ṣaḥīḥ al-Jāmiʿ* 6518)

j. Be kind and Allah will be kind to you

Ibn Ḥibbān (رحمه الله) reported: ʿUmar ibn ʿAbd al-ʿAzīz (رحمه الله) said:

أَحَبُّ الْأُمُورِ إِلَى اللَّهِ ثَلَاثَةٌ الْعَفْوُ فِي الْقُدْرَةِ وَالْقَصْدُ فِي الْجِدَّةِ وَالرِّفْقُ فِي الْعِبَادَةِ وَمَا رَفَقَ أَحَدٌ بِأَحَدٍ فِي الدُّنْيَا إِلَّا رَفَقَ اللَّهُ بِهِ يَوْمَ الْقِيَامَة

"The most beloved matters to Allah are three: forgiveness in a position of power; moderation in a position of affluence; and gentleness in worship. No one is kind to another in this world but that Allah will be gentle with him on the Day of Resurrection." (*Rawḍat al-ʿUqalāʾ* 1/167)

k. Visiting a man only for the sake of Allah

Anas ibn Mālik (رضي الله عنه) reported: The Prophet (ﷺ) said:

أَلَا أُخْبِرُكُمْ بِرِجَالِكُمْ فِي الْجَنَّةِ قُلْنَا بَلَى يَا رَسُولَ اللَّهِ قَالَ النَّبِيُّ فِي الْجَنَّةِ وَالصِّدِّيقُ فِي الْجَنَّةِ وَالشَّهِيدُ فِي الْجَنَّةِ وَالْمَوْلُودُ فِي الْجَنَّةِ وَالرَّجُلُ يَزُورُ أَخَاهُ فِي نَاحِيَةِ الْمِصْرِ لَا يَزُورُهُ إِلَّا لِلَّهِ فِي الْجَنَّةِ

"Shall I not tell you about the best of your men?" We said: "Of course, O Messenger of Allah." The Prophet (ﷺ) said: "The Prophet is in *Jannah*, the truthful are in *Jannah*, the martyrs are in *Jannah*, the child who dies is in *Jannah*, and a man who visits his brother in a faraway land, only visiting him for the sake of Allah, is in *Jannah*." (*al-Muʿjam al-Kabīr* 1743, Ḥasan li-ghayrihī (authentic due to external evidences), according to al-Albānī)

Anas ibn Mālik (رضي الله عنه) reported: The Prophet (ﷺ) said:

مَا مِنْ عَبْدٍ مُسْلِمٍ أَتَى أَخًا لَهُ يَزُورُهُ فِي اللَّهِ إِلاَّ نَادَاهُ مُنَادٍ مِنَ السَّمَاءِ أَنْ طِبْتَ وَطَابَتْ لَكَ الْجَنَّةُ وَإِلَّا قَالَ اللَّهُ فِي مَلَكُوتِ عَرْشِهِ عَبْدِي زَارَ فِيَّ وَعَلَيَّ قِرَاهُ فَلَمْ يَرْضَ اللَّهُ لَهُ بِثَوَابٍ دُونَ الْجَنَّةِ

"No *muslim* servant visits his brother for the sake of Allah but that a caller from the heavens announces: 'You are purified and *Jannah* is purified for you!' Otherwise, Allah says in the realms of His throne: 'My servant has visited Me and his guest for My sake, so I am not pleased for him to have any reward other than *Jannah*.' " (*Musnad al-Bazzār* 6466, *Ḥasan li-ghayrihī* (authentic due to external evidences), according to al-Albānī)

l. ***Easy-going people will be in Jannah***

Ibn Masʿūd (رضي الله عنه) reported: The Messenger of Allah (ﷺ) said:

أَلَا أُخْبِرُكُمْ بِمَنْ يَحْرُمُ عَلَى النَّارِ أَوْ بِمَنْ تَحْرُمُ عَلَيْهِ النَّارُ عَلَى كُلِّ قَرِيبٍ هَيِّنٍ سَهْلٍ

"Shall I not tell you of one forbidden for *Jahannam* or *Jahannam* is forbidden for him? It is everyone accessible, polite, and easy-going." (*Sunan al-Tirmidhī* 2488, *Ṣaḥīḥ li gharyihī* (authentic due to external evidence) according to al-Albānī)

Abū Hurayrah (رضي الله عنه) reported: The Prophet (ﷺ) said:

مَنْ كَانَ لَيِّنًا هَيِّنًا سَهْلًا حَرَّمَهُ اللهُ عَلَى النَّارِ

"Whoever is kind, friendly, and easy-going, Allah will forbid him from entering *Jahannam*." (*al-Sunan al-Kubrā lil-Bayhaqī* 20806, *Ṣaḥīḥ* according to al-Albānī)

Ibn al-Muntafiq (رضي الله عنه) reported:

I said: "O Messenger of Allah, teach me what will save me from the punishment of Allah and admit me into *Jannah*." The Messenger of Allah (ﷺ) said:

اعْبُدِ اللَّهَ وَلا تُشْرِكْ بِهِ شَيْئًا وَأَقِمِ الصَّلاةَ الْمَكْتُوبَةَ وَأَدِّ الزَّكَاةَ الْمَفْرُوضَةَ وَحُجَّ وَاعْتَمِرْ وَصُمْ رَمَضَانَ وَانْظُرْ مَا تُحِبُّ لِلنَّاسِ أَنْ يَأْتُوهُ إِلَيْكَ فَافْعَلْهُ بِهِمْ وَمَا تَكْرَهُ أَنْ يَأْتُوهُ إِلَيْكَ فَذَرْهُمْ مِنْهُ

"Worship Allah and do not associate anything with Him, establish the prescribed prayers, give the obligatory charity, perform the Hajj and ʿ*umrah* pilgrimages, and fast the month of *Ramaḍān*. Look at the way you would love people to treat you and do so to them, and whatever you would hate for them to do to you, spare them of it." (*al-Muʿjam al-Kabīr lil-Ṭabarānī* 19/210, *Ṣaḥīḥ* according to al-Albānī)

ʿAbdullāh ibn ʿAmr (رضي الله عنه) reported: The Messenger of Allah (ﷺ) said:

إِنَّ فِي الْجَنَّةِ غُرْفَةً يُرَى ظَاهِرُهَا مِنْ بَاطِنِهَا وَبَاطِنُهَا مِنْ ظَاهِرِهَا فَقَالَ أَبُو مُوسَى الْأَشْعَرِيُّ لِمَنْ هِيَ يَا رَسُولَ اللَّهِ قَالَ لِمَنْ أَلَانَ الْكَلَامَ وَأَطْعَمَ الطَّعَامَ وَبَاتَ لِلَّهِ قَائِمًا وَالنَّاسُ نِيَامٌ

"Verily, in *Jannah* are rooms whose outside can be seen from inside and whose inside can be seen from outside." Abū Mūsā (رضي الله عنه) said: "Who are they for, O Messenger of Allah?" The Prophet (ﷺ) said: "For those who speak mildly, feed the hungry, and spend the night standing for the sake of Allah while people sleep." (*Sunan al-Tirmidhī* 1984, *Musnad Aḥmad* 6436, *Ṣaḥīḥ* according to Aḥmad Shākir)

m. ***Whoever leaves arguing will have a house in Jannah***

Abū Umāmah (رضي الله عنه) reported: The Messenger of Allah (ﷺ) said:

أَنَا زَعِيمٌ بِبَيْتٍ فِي رَبَضِ الْجَنَّةِ لِمَنْ تَرَكَ الْمِرَاءَ وَإِنْ كَانَ مُحِقًّا وَبِبَيْتٍ فِي وَسَطِ الْجَنَّةِ لِمَنْ تَرَكَ الْكَذِبَ وَإِنْ كَانَ مَازِحًا وَبِبَيْتٍ فِي أَعْلَى الْجَنَّةِ لِمَنْ حَسَّنَ خُلُقَهُ

"I guarantee a house on the outskirts of *Jannah* for one who leaves arguments even if he is right, and a house in the middle of *Jannah* for one who abandons lies even when joking, and a house in the highest part of *Jannah* for one who makes his character excellent." (*Sunan Abī Dāwūd* 4800, *Ṣaḥīḥ* according to al-Nawawī)

n. *Not backbiting will earn you Jannah*

ʿĀʾishah (﷠) reported: The Prophet (ﷺ) said:

خِصَالٌ سِتٌّ مَا مِنْ مُسْلِمٍ يَمُوتُ فِي وَاحِدَةٍ مِنْهُنَّ إِلا كَانَ ضَامِنًا عَلَى اللَّهِ أَنْ يُدْخِلَهُ الْجَنَّةَ رَجُلٌ خَرَجَ مُجَاهِدًا فَإِنْ مَاتَ فِي وَجْهِهِ كَانَ ضَامِنًا عَلَى اللَّهِ وَرَجُلٌ تَبِعَ جَنَازَةً فَإِنْ مَاتَ فِي وَجْهِهِ كَانَ ضَامِنًا عَلَى اللَّهِ وَرَجُلٌ عَادَ مَرِيضًا فَإِنْ مَاتَ فِي وَجْهِهِ كَانَ ضَامِنًا عَلَى اللَّهِ وَرَجُلٌ تَوَضَّأَ فَأَحْسَنَ الْوُضُوءَ ثُمَّ خَرَجَ إِلَى مَسْجِدٍ لِصَلاتِهِ فَإِنْ مَاتَ فِي وَجْهِهِ كَانَ ضَامِنًا عَلَى اللَّهِ وَرَجُلٌ أَتَى إِمَامًا لا يَأْتِيهِ إِلا لِيُعَزِّرَهُ وَيُوَقِّرَهُ فَإِنْ مَاتَ فِي وَجْهِهِ ذَلِكَ كَانَ ضَامِنًا عَلَى اللَّهِ وَرَجُلٌ فِي بَيْتِهِ لا يَغْتَابُ مُسْلِمًا وَلا يَجُرُّ إِلَيْهِ سَخَطًا وَلا يَنْقِمُهُ فَإِنْ مَاتَ فِي وَجْهِهِ كَانَ ضَامِنًا عَلَى اللَّهِ

"No *muslim* dies with one of six traits but that he has a guarantee from Allah he will be admitted into *Jannah*. A man who goes out for jihad; if he dies in this state, his guarantee is upon Allah. A man who follows a funeral procession; if he dies in this state, his guarantee is upon Allah. A man who visits a sick person; if he dies in this state, his guarantee is upon Allah. A man who performs ablution in the best manner and then goes out to the *masjid* for his prayer; if he dies in this state, his guarantee is upon Allah. A man who comes to a *muslim* leader for no reason but to honor and respect him; if he dies in this state, his guarantee is upon Allah. A man in his house who does not backbite a *muslim* and he does not bring displeasure or vengeance upon himself; if he dies in this state, his guarantee is upon Allah." (*al-Muʿjam al-Awsaṭ* 3948, *Ṣaḥīḥ li-ghayrihī* (authentic due to external evidence), according to al-Albānī)

o. *Loving the believers will make you be at the right side of the Throne*

Ibn ʿAbbās (ﷺ) reported: The Prophet (ﷺ) said:

إِنَّ لِلَّهِ جُلَسَاءَ يَوْمَ الْقِيَامَةِ عَنْ يَمِينِ الْعَرْشِ وَكِلْتَا يَدَيِ اللَّهِ يَمِينٌ عَلَى مَنَابِرَ مِنْ نُورٍ وُجُوهُهُمْ مِنْ نُورٍ لَيْسُوا بِأَنْبِيَاءَ وَلا شُهَدَاءَ وَلا صِدِّيقِينَ قِيلَ يَا رَسُولَ اللَّهِ مَنْ هُمْ قَالَ الْمُتَحَابُّونَ بِجِلالِ اللَّهِ تَعَالَى

"Verily, Allah will have an audience on the Day of Resurrection, sitting on the right side of His Throne, and both sides are honored as the right. They will be upon pulpits of light and there will be light upon their faces, yet they are not prophets, nor martyrs, nor disciples." It was said: "O Messenger of Allah, who are they?" The Prophet (ﷺ) said: "Those who loved each other for the glory of Allah the Almighty." (*al-Muʿjam al-Kabīr lil-Ṭabarānī* 12686, *Ṣaḥīḥ* according to al-Albānī)

ʿIyāḍ ibn Ḥimār (ﷺ) reported: The Messenger of Allah (ﷺ) said:

وَأَهْلُ الْجَنَّةِ ثَلاثَةٌ ذُو سُلْطَانٍ مُقْسِطٌ مُتَصَدِّقٌ مُوَفَّقٌ وَرَجُلٌ رَحِيمٌ رَقِيقُ الْقَلْبِ لِكُلِّ ذِي قُرْبَى وَمُسْلِمٍ وَعَفِيفٌ مُتَعَفِّفٌ ذُو عِيَالٍ

"The people of *Jannah* are three kinds: an authority who is fair, truthful, and guided; a man who has mercy and kindness in his heart towards his relatives and every *muslim*; and one who refuses to beg although he has dependents." (*Ṣaḥīḥ Muslim* 2865)

p. Being just will earn you entrance into Jannah

Abū Hurayrah (رضي الله عنه) reported: The Messenger of Allah (ﷺ) said:

مَنْ طَلَبَ قَضَاءَ الْمُسْلِمِينَ حَتَّى يَنَالَهُ ثُمَّ غَلَبَ عَدْلُهُ جَوْرَهُ فَلَهُ الْجَنَّةُ وَمَنْ غَلَبَ جَوْرُهُ عَدْلَهُ فَلَهُ النَّارُ

"Whoever seeks to be a judge over the *muslims* such that he acquires it and his justice outweighs his tyranny, he will have *Jannah*. If his tyranny outweighs his justice, he will have *Jahannam*." (*Sunan Abī Dāwūd* 3575, *Ḥasan* according to Ibn Kathīr)

Abū Saʿīd al-Khudrī (رضي الله عنه) reported: The Messenger of Allah (ﷺ) said:

يَخْلُصُ الْمُؤْمِنُونَ مِنَ النَّارِ فَيُحْبَسُونَ عَلَى قَنْطَرَةٍ بَيْنَ الْجَنَّةِ وَالنَّارِ فَيُقَصُّ لِبَعْضِهِمْ مِنْ بَعْضٍ مَظَالِمُ كَانَتْ بَيْنَهُمْ فِي الدُّنْيَا حَتَّى إِذَا هُذِّبُوا وَنُقُّوا أُذِنَ لَهُمْ فِي دُخُولِ الْجَنَّةِ فَوَالَّذِي نَفْسُ مُحَمَّدٍ بِيَدِهِ لَأَحَدُهُمْ أَهْدَى بِمَنْزِلِهِ فِي الْجَنَّةِ مِنْهُ بِمَنْزِلِهِ كَانَ فِي الدُّنْيَا

"The believers will be saved from *Jahannam* and they will be stopped at a bridge between *Jannah* and *Jahannam*. Then, they will justly retaliate against each other for wrongs committed between them in the world, until they are cleansed and purified for admittance into *Jannah*. By the One in whose hand is the soul of Muhammad, one of you will know his residence in *Jannah* better than his residence in the world." (*Ṣaḥīḥ al-Bukhārī* 6535)

q. *The killed and killer will enter Jannah*

Abū Hurayrah (ﷺ) reported: The Messenger of Allah (ﷺ) said:

يَضْحَكُ اللَّهُ إِلَى رَجُلَيْنِ يَقْتُلُ أَحَدُهُمَا الْآخَرَ يَدْخُلَانِ الْجَنَّةَ يُقَاتِلُ هَذَا فِي سَبِيلِ اللَّهِ فَيُقْتَلُ ثُمَّ يَتُوبُ اللَّهُ عَلَى الْقَاتِلِ فَيُسْتَشْهَدُ

"Allah laughs at two men; one of them killed the other, yet they both entered *Jannah*. This one fought in the way of Allah and was killed, then his killer repented and was also martyred." (*Ṣaḥīḥ al-Bukhārī* 2671, *Ṣaḥīḥ Muslim* 1890)

r. *Loving for the sake of Allah will earn you Jannah*

ʿAbdullah ibn ʿAmr (ﷺ) reported: The Messenger of Allah (ﷺ) said:

مَنْ أَحَبَّ رَجُلًا لِلَّهِ فَقَالَ إِنِّي أُحِبُّكَ لِلَّهِ فَدَخَلَا الْجَنَّةَ فَكَانَ الَّذِي أَحَبَّ أَرْفَعُ مَنْزِلَةً مِنَ الْآخَرِ أُلْحِقَ بِالَّذِي أَحَبَّ لِلَّهِ

"Whoever loves a man for the sake of Allah, then he should say: 'I love you for the sake of Allah.' They will both enter *Jannah* together. He whose love is greater will be raised in status over the other; he will be joined with the one he loved for the sake of Allah." (*Musnad al-Bazzār* 2439, *Ḥasan* according to al-Haythamī)

Abū Saʿīd al-Khudrī (ﷺ) reported: The Messenger of Allah (ﷺ) said:

إِنَّ الْمُتَحَابِّينَ لَتُرَى غُرَفُهُمْ فِي الْجَنَّةِ كَالْكَوْكَبِ الطَّالِعِ الشَّرْقِيِّ أَوْ الْغَرْبِيِّ فَيُقَالُ مَنْ هَؤُلَاءِ فَيُقَالُ هَؤُلَاءِ الْمُتَحَابُّونَ فِي اللَّهِ عَزَّ وَجَلَّ

"Verily, those who loved each other will have chambers in *Jannah* that are seen as if they were rising stars in the east or west. It will be said: 'Who are these people?' Thus it will be said: 'They are those who loved each other for the sake of Allah the Almighty.' " (*Musnad Aḥmad* 11829, *Rijāl al-Ṣaḥīḥ* (narrators reliable) according to al-Haythamī)

s. *Greeting each other will earn you Jannah*

Abū Umāmah (ﷺ) reported: The Messenger of Allah (ﷺ) said:

ثَلاثَةٌ كُلُّهُمْ ضَامِنٌ عَلَى اللَّهِ إِنْ عَاشَ رُزِقَ وَكُفِيَ وَإِنْ مَاتَ أَدْخَلَهُ اللَّهُ الْجَنَّةَ مَنْ دَخَلَ بَيْتَهُ فَسَلَّمَ فَهُوَ ضَامِنٌ عَلَى اللَّهِ وَمَنْ خَرَجَ إِلَى الْمَسْجِدِ فَهُوَ ضَامِنٌ عَلَى اللَّهِ وَمَنْ خَرَجَ فِي سَبِيلِ اللَّهِ فَهُوَ ضَامِنٌ عَلَى اللَّهِ

"Three people have a guarantee from Allah. If he lives he will have provision to suffice him, and if he dies he will enter *Jannah*: one who enters and greets with peace has a guarantee from Allah; one who goes out to the *masjid* has a guarantee from Allah; and one who goes out in the way of Allah has a guarantee from Allah." (*Ṣaḥīḥ Ibn Ḥibbān* 504, *Ṣaḥīḥ* according to al-Mundhirī)

Bab al-Kāẓimīn, where forgiveness shines so bright,
In hearts that pardon, there's a heavenly light.

Allah's mercy graces those who debts forgave,
Jan*nah* they will find for what they humbly gave.

Forgive others, Allah's pardon will accrue,
In Paradise's grace, His love for you anew.

Those who reconcile, Allah will surely raise,
In *Jannah*'s heights, they find eternal praise.

Suppressing anger, *Jahannam*'s flames they shun,
In Allah's sight, their deeds are nobly done.

Most beloved to Allah, their souls embrace,
In *Jannah*'s gardens, they find their rightful place.

Whoever controls anger finds security and faith,
In *Jannah*'s realms, they'll find their blessed wraith.

Content on Judgment Day, Allah's grace bestowed,
In *Jannah*'s gardens, by rivers, they'll be stowed.

Ḥūr al-ʿAyn, in Paradise's radiant gleam,
For those who forgive, they'll fulfil their dream.

Be kind, and Allah's kindness shall come to you,
In *Jannah*'s bliss, His love forever true.

Visiting for His sake, in friendship's array,
In Paradise's light, they'll find their way.

Easy-going souls, in *Jannah*'s gardens bloom,
In peace and harmony, they'll find their room.

Leaving arguments behind, their hearts are free,
In *Jannah*'s mansions, they're meant to be.

No backbiting tongues, in *Jannah* they're adorned,
In Paradise's beauty, they're forever sworn.

Loving the believers, by the Throne they'll stand,
In Allah's favour, on the right side's land.

Justice they uphold, their hearts pure and clean,
In *Jannah*'s grace, their souls shall convene.

The killer and the killed, in *Jannah*'s embrace,
Their souls find peace, in Allah's loving grace.

Loving for His sake, in *Jannah*'s light they'll glow,
In Paradise's love, their hearts forever aglow.

Greeting each other, with love and harmony,
In *Jannah*'s blessings, they'll forever be.

CHAPTER

Nine

BĀB AL-WĀLID

GATE OF THE FATHER
(MIDDLE GATE)

This gate is for those who respect, honour, and are righteous to their parents, specifically to their father.

وَٱعْبُدُوا۟ ٱللَّهَ وَلَا تُشْرِكُوا۟ بِهِۦ شَيْـًٔا ۖ وَبِٱلْوَٰلِدَيْنِ إِحْسَـٰنًا ﴿٣٦﴾

"Worship Allah and associate nothing with Him, and be good to parents." (*al-Nisāʾ*, 4:36)

قُلْ تَعَالَوْا۟ أَتْلُ مَا حَرَّمَ رَبُّكُمْ عَلَيْكُمْ ۖ أَلَّا تُشْرِكُوا۟ بِهِۦ شَيْـًٔا ۖ وَبِٱلْوَٰلِدَيْنِ إِحْسَـٰنًا ۖ ﴿١٥١﴾

"Say: Come, I will recite what your Lord has made sacred to you. He commands that you do not associate anything with Him and be good to your parents." (*al-Anʿām*, 6:151)

وَقَضَىٰ رَبُّكَ أَلَّا تَعْبُدُوٓا۟ إِلَّآ إِيَّاهُ وَبِٱلْوَٰلِدَيْنِ إِحْسَـٰنًا ۚ إِمَّا يَبْلُغَنَّ عِندَكَ ٱلْكِبَرَ أَحَدُهُمَآ أَوْ كِلَاهُمَا فَلَا تَقُل لَّهُمَآ أُفٍّ وَلَا تَنْهَرْهُمَا وَقُل لَّهُمَا قَوْلًا كَرِيمًا ﴿٢٣﴾ وَٱخْفِضْ لَهُمَا جَنَاحَ ٱلذُّلِّ مِنَ ٱلرَّحْمَةِ وَقُل رَّبِّ ٱرْحَمْهُمَا كَمَا رَبَّيَانِى صَغِيرًا ﴿٢٤﴾

"Your Lord has decreed that you worship none but Him and be good to your parents. Whether one or both of them reach old age with you, do not say to them a word of annoyance and do not repel them, but rather speak to them a noble word. Lower to them the wing of humility out of mercy, and say: My Lord, have mercy upon them as they brought me up when I was small." (*al-Isrāʾ*, 17:23-24)

وَوَصَّيْنَا ٱلْإِنسَـٰنَ بِوَٰلِدَيْهِ حَمَلَتْهُ أُمُّهُۥ وَهْنًا عَلَىٰ وَهْنٍ وَفِصَـٰلُهُۥ فِى عَامَيْنِ أَنِ ٱشْكُرْ لِى وَلِوَٰلِدَيْكَ إِلَىَّ ٱلْمَصِيرُ ﴿١٤﴾ وَإِن جَـٰهَدَاكَ عَلَىٰٓ أَن تُشْرِكَ بِى مَا لَيْسَ لَكَ بِهِۦ عِلْمٌ فَلَا تُطِعْهُمَا ۖ وَصَاحِبْهُمَا فِى ٱلدُّنْيَا مَعْرُوفًا ۖ وَٱتَّبِعْ سَبِيلَ مَنْ أَنَابَ إِلَىَّ ۚ ثُمَّ إِلَىَّ مَرْجِعُكُمْ فَأُنَبِّئُكُم بِمَا كُنتُمْ تَعْمَلُونَ ﴿١٥﴾

"And We have enjoined upon man [care] for his parents. His mother carried him, [increasing her] in weakness upon weakness, and his weaning is in two years. Be grateful to Me and to your parents; to Me is the [final] destination. If they strive to make you associate with Me that of which you have no knowledge, then do not obey them but accompany them in this world with appropriate kindness and follow the way of those who turn back to Me." (*Luqmān*, 31:14-15)

a. *The father is the middle gate of Jannah*

Abū al-Dardāʾ (ﷺ) reported: The Prophet (ﷺ) said:

الْوَالِدُ أَوْسَطُ أَبْوَابِ الْجَنَّةِ فَإِنْ شِئْتَ فَأَضِعْ ذَلِكَ الْبَابَ أَوْ احْفَظْهُ

"The father[5] is the middle of the gates of *Jannah*, so keep to this gate or lose it." (*Sunan al-Tirmidhī* 1900, *Ṣaḥīḥ*)

b. *The best act of righteousness*

ʿAbdullāh ibn ʿUmar (ﷺ) reported: The Prophet (ﷺ) said:

أَبَرُّ الْبِرِّ أَنْ يَصِلَ الرَّجُلُ وُدَّ أَبِيهِ

"The best act of righteousness is to maintain relations with a man loved by his father." (*Ṣaḥīḥ Muslim* 2552)

c. *The Prophets and the righteous have pure hearts*

Abū Hurayrah (ﷺ) narrates that the Prophet (ﷺ) said:

إِنَّ اللَّهَ عَزَّ وَجَلَّ لَيَرْفَعُ الدَّرَجَةَ لِلْعَبْدِ الصَّالِحِ فِي الْجَنَّةِ فَيَقُولُ يَا رَبِّ أَنَّى لِي هَذِهِ فَيَقُولُ بِاسْتِغْفَارِ وَلَدِكَ لَكَ

"Verily, Allah the Almighty will raise the status of his righteous servants in *Jannah* and they will say: 'O Lord, what is this?' Allah will say: 'This is due to your child seeking forgiveness for you.' " (*Musnad Aḥmad* 10232, *Ḥasan* according to al-Arnāʾūṭ)

5 In some of the commentary of the scholars, it is not specific to the father but to the parents in general. The author decided to give the apparent, literal translation of the *ḥadīth*.

d. No child can repay his father

Abū Hurayrah (ﷺ) reported: The Messenger of Allah (ﷺ) said:

لا يَجْزِي وَلَدٌ وَالِدًا إِلَّا أَنْ يَجِدَهُ مَمْلُوكًا فَيَشْتَرِيَهُ فَيُعْتِقَهُ

"No child can compensate his father unless he finds him as a slave, buys him, and sets him free." (*Ṣaḥīḥ Muslim* 1510)

e. Jannah is with your mother

Muᶜāwiyah ibn Jāhimah (ﷺ) reported: Jāhimah came to the Messenger of Allah (ﷺ) and said: "O Messenger of Allah, I intend to join the expedition and I seek your advice." The Prophet (ﷺ) said:

هَلْ لَكَ مِنْ أُمٍّ

"Do you have a mother? He said: "Yes." The Prophet (ﷺ) said:

فَالْزَمْهَا فَإِنَّ الْجَنَّةَ تَحْتَ رِجْلَيْهَا

"Stay with her, for *Jannah* is beneath her feet." (*Sunan al-Nasāʾī* 3104, *Ṣaḥīḥ* according to al-Albānī)

f. Obeying and honouring is a means to entering Jannah

Abū Hurayrah (ﷺ) that the Prophet (ﷺ) said:

رَغِمَ أَنْفُ، ثم رَغِمَ أَنْفُ، ثم رَغِمَ أَنْفُ

"He is doomed, he is doomed, he is doomed."

It was said: "Allah's Messenger, who is he?" He said:

مَنْ أَدْرَكَ أَبَوَيْهِ عِنْدَ الْكِبَرِ أَحَدَهُمَا أَوْ كِلَيْهِمَا فَلَمْ يَدْخُلِ الْجَنَّةَ

"Whoever finds his parents, one or both of them, reach old age during his lifetime but he does not enter *Jannah*." (*Ṣaḥīḥ Muslim*, 2551a)

g. *Being good to your mother is the best deed*

ʿAṭāʾ ibn Yasār (ﷺ) reported: A man came to Ibn ʿAbbās (ﷺ) and said: "I proposed to a woman and she refused to marry me. Another man proposed to her and she was happy to marry him. I became jealous and I killed her. Is there any repentance for me?" Ibn ʿAbbās said: "Is your mother alive?" The man said: "No." Ibn ʿAbbās said: "Repent to Allah the Almighty and draw close to him in worship as much as you can." I went to Ibn ʿAbbās and I asked him: "Why did you ask if his mother was alive?" Ibn ʿAbbās said: "Verily, I do not know of any deed better to bring one closer to Allah the Almighty than goodness to one's mother." (*al-Adab al-Mufrad* 4, *Ṣaḥīḥ* according to Al-Albānī)

A poet once wrote:[6]

أغرى امرُؤٌ يومًا غلامًا جاهلا

بنقوده كي ما ينالَ به الوطر

قال ائتني بفؤاد أمك يا فتى

ولك الجواهرُ والدراهمُ والدرر

فمضى وأغمد خِنجَرًا في صدرها

والقلبَ أخرجه وعاد على الأثر

لكنه من فَرطِ سرعته هوى

فتدحرج القلبُ المقَطَّعُ إذ عثر

ناده قلبُ الأم وهو مُعَفَّرٌ

6 Ibrāhīm al-Mundhir.

ولدي حبيبي هل أصابك من ضرر؟

فكأن هذا الصوتَ رُغمَ حُنُوِّه

غضبُ السماء على الغلام قد انهمر

فَدَرى فَظِيعَ جنايةٍ لم يجنها

ولدٌ سواه منذُ تاريخِ البشر

فارتد نحو القلبِ يَغسِله بما

سالت بها عيناه من فَيضِ العِبَر

ويقول يا قلب انتقم مني ولا

تَغفر فإن جريمتي لا تُغتَفَر

واستلَّ خِنجَره ليطعنَ نفسه

طعناً فيبقى عبرةً لمن اعتُبر

ناداه قلبُ الأم كف يدًا ولا

تذبَح فؤادي مرتين على الأثر

"One day, a man tempted an ignorant boy with his money to safeguard it against harm.

'Bring me the heart of your mother, O boy,

And to you I will give jewels, gold, and pearls.'

So, the boy went and struck a dagger into his mother's chest,

And took out the heart and went back the way he came.

But because of his excessive haste,

He fell and so did the torn heart and rolled as he stumbled.

The mother's heart called out to him while being covered in dust,

'My Son! My Beloved! Are you okay?!'

And suddenly, even though the voice was very compassionate, it was as if

The wrath of the heavens had fallen upon him.

And he realised the heinous nature of his crime which none has committed

Before him in the history of mankind.

So, he returned back to the heart to wash it,

With what flowed from his eyes; tears in abundance.

And he said: 'O heart! Take revenge on me and do not,

Forgive, for my crime is unforgiveable!'

So, he unsheathed his dagger to stab himself

A stabbing to become an example for those who heed example.

The mother's heart called out to him: 'Stop your hand! And do not

Stab my heart twice in the same place!' "

Bāb al-Wālid, where love and honour reside,
In the middle gate, our hearts find their guide.

The father, a gate to *Jannah*'s embrace,
His love and guidance, a heavenly grace.

The best act of righteousness, to parents be true,
In *Jannah*'s gardens, Allah's love shines through.

No child can repay, what a father has given,
In Allah's mercy, their hearts are forgiven.

Jannah, too, with your mother, you'll find,
Her love and care, forever intertwined.

Obeying and honouring parents, a path so clear,
In Paradise's beauty, they forever draw near.

Bāb al-Wālid, in family's love and care,
In *Jannah*'s gates, your place is so fair.

CHAPTER Ten

BĀB AL-TAWBAH

GATE OF REPENTANCE[7]

7 According to Imam al-Nawawī (ﷺ).

This is a gate of *Jannah* for those who are always repenting to Allah.

سَابِقُوٓاْ إِلَىٰ مَغْفِرَةٍ مِّن رَّبِّكُمْ وَجَنَّةٍ عَرْضُهَا كَعَرْضِ ٱلسَّمَآءِ وَٱلْأَرْضِ أُعِدَّتْ لِلَّذِينَ ءَامَنُواْ بِٱللَّهِ وَرُسُلِهِۦ ۚ ذَٰلِكَ فَضْلُ ٱللَّهِ يُؤْتِيهِ مَن يَشَآءُ ۚ وَٱللَّهُ ذُو ٱلْفَضْلِ ٱلْعَظِيمِ ﴿٢١﴾

"Compete with one another for forgiveness from your Lord and a *Jannah* as vast as the heavens and the earth, prepared for those who believe in Allah and His messengers. This is the favour of Allah. He grants it to whoever He wills. And Allah is the Lord of infinite bounty." (*al-Ḥadīd*, 57:21)

وَتُوبُوٓاْ إِلَى ٱللَّهِ جَمِيعًا أَيُّهَ ٱلْمُؤْمِنُونَ لَعَلَّكُمْ تُفْلِحُونَ ﴿٣١﴾

"Turn to Allah in repentance all together, O believers, so that you may be successful." (*al-Nūr*, 24:31)

يَٰٓأَيُّهَا ٱلَّذِينَ ءَامَنُواْ تُوبُوٓاْ إِلَى ٱللَّهِ تَوْبَةً نَّصُوحًا عَسَىٰ رَبُّكُمْ أَن يُكَفِّرَ عَنكُمْ سَيِّـَٔاتِكُمْ وَيُدْخِلَكُمْ جَنَّٰتٍ تَجْرِى مِن تَحْتِهَا ٱلْأَنْهَٰرُ يَوْمَ لَا يُخْزِى ٱللَّهُ ٱلنَّبِىَّ وَٱلَّذِينَ ءَامَنُواْ مَعَهُۥ ۖ نُورُهُمْ يَسْعَىٰ بَيْنَ أَيْدِيهِمْ وَبِأَيْمَٰنِهِمْ يَقُولُونَ رَبَّنَآ أَتْمِمْ لَنَا نُورَنَا وَٱغْفِرْ لَنَآ ۖ إِنَّكَ عَلَىٰ كُلِّ شَىْءٍ قَدِيرٌ ﴿٨﴾

"O believers! Turn to Allah in sincere repentance, so your Lord may absolve you of your sins and admit you into Gardens, under which rivers flow, on the Day Allah will not disgrace the Prophet or the believers with him. Their light will shine ahead of them and on their right. They will say: 'Our Lord! Perfect our light for us, and forgive us. [For] You are truly Most Capable of everything.' " (*al-Taḥrīm*, 66:8)

قُلْ يَٰعِبَادِىَ ٱلَّذِينَ أَسْرَفُواْ عَلَىٰٓ أَنفُسِهِمْ لَا تَقْنَطُواْ مِن رَّحْمَةِ ٱللَّهِ ۚ إِنَّ ٱللَّهَ يَغْفِرُ ٱلذُّنُوبَ جَمِيعًا ۚ إِنَّهُۥ هُوَ ٱلْغَفُورُ ٱلرَّحِيمُ ﴿٥٣﴾

"Say: [O Prophet, that Allah says,] O My servants who have exceeded the limits against their souls! Do not lose hope in Allah's mercy, for Allah certainly forgives all sins. He is indeed the All-Forgiving, Most Merciful." (*al-Zumar*, 39:53)

a. He enters Jannah because he never forgot his sins

Hishām ibn Ḥassān (ﷺ) reported: al-Ḥasan al-Baṣrī (ﷺ) said:

إِنَّ الرَّجُلَ يُذْنِبُ الذَّنْبَ فَمَا يَنْسَاهُ وَمَا يَزَالُ مُتَخَوِّفًا مِنْهُ حَتَّى يَدْخُلَ الْجَنَّةَ

"Verily, a man may commit a sin and he never forgets it, always fearing it, until he enters *Jannah*." (*al-Zuhd li-Aḥmad ibn Ḥanbal* 1581)

b. Allah loves repentance

Abū Ayyūb (ﷺ) narrates: The Messenger of Allah (ﷺ) said:

لَوْلَا أَنَّكُمْ تُذْنِبُونَ لَخَلَقَ اللَّهُ خَلْقًا يُذْنِبُونَ يَغْفِرُ لَهُمْ

"If you were not to sin, Allah would certainly create people who would sin and He would forgive them." (*Ṣaḥīḥ Muslim* 2748)

c. Prophets and the righteous have pure hearts

Abū Nuʿaym (ﷺ) reported: Fuḍayl ibn ʿIyāḍ (ﷺ) said:

كَانَ يُقَالُ مِنْ أَخْلَاقِ الأَنْبِيَاءِ وَالأَصْفِيَاءِ الأَخْيَارِ الطَّاهِرَةِ قُلُوبُهُمْ خَلائِقُ ثَلاثَةٌ الْحِلْمُ وَالإِنَابةُ وَحَظٌّ مِنْ قِيَامِ اللَّيْلِ

"It has been said that among the character of the Prophets and chosen elect is the purity of their hearts. They are three characteristics: forbearance, penitence, and a portion of prayer in the night." (*Ḥilyat al-Awliyāʾ* 11718)

d. ***Allah laughs at two types of people in Jannah***

Abū Hurayrah (ﷺ) reported: The Messenger of Allah (ﷺ) said:

يَضْحَكُ اللَّهُ إِلَى رَجُلَيْنِ يَقْتُلُ أَحَدُهُمَا الْآخَرَ يَدْخُلَانِ الْجَنَّةَ يُقَاتِلُ هَذَا فِي سَبِيلِ اللَّهِ فَيُقْتَلُ ثُمَّ يَتُوبُ اللَّهُ عَلَى الْقَاتِلِ فَيُسْتَشْهَدُ

"Allah laughs at two men; one of them killed the other yet they both entered *Jannah*. This one fought in the way of Allah and was killed, then his killer repented and was also martyred." (*Ṣaḥīḥ al-Bukhārī* 2671, *Ṣaḥīḥ Muslim* 1890)

e. ***Blessed is the one who seeks forgiveness often***

ʿAbdullāh ibn Busr (ﷺ) reported: The Prophet (ﷺ) said:

طُوبَى لِمَنْ وَجَدَ فِي صَحِيفَتِهِ اسْتِغْفَارًا كَثِيرًا

"Glad tidings to the one who finds much repentance in his record." (*Sunan Ibn Mājah* 3818, *Ṣaḥīḥ* according to al-Suyūṭī)

f. ***Allah never tires of forgiving***

عَنْ عُقْبَةَ بْنِ عَامِرٍ أَنَّ رَجُلا أَتَى رَسُولَ اللَّهِ صَلَّى اللَّهُ عَلَيْهِ وَسَلَّمَ فَقَالَ يَا رَسُولَ اللَّهِ أَحَدُنَا يُذْنِبُ قَالَ يُكْتَبُ عَلَيْهِ قَالَ ثُمَّ يَسْتَغْفِرُ مِنْهُ وَيَتُوبُ قَالَ يُغْفَرُ لَهُ وَيُتَابُ عَلَيْهِ قَالَ فَيَعُودُ فَيُذْنِبُ قَالَ يُكْتَبُ عَلَيْهِ قَالَ ثُمَّ يَسْتَغْفِرُ مِنْهُ وَيَتُوبُ قَالَ يُغْفَرُ لَهُ وَيُتَابُ عَلَيْهِ وَلا يَمَلُّ اللَّهُ حَتَّى تَمَلُّو

ʿUqbah ibn ʿĀmir (ﷺ) reported:

A man came to the Messenger of Allah (ﷺ) and he said: "O Messenger of Allah, one of us has committed a sin." The Prophet (ﷺ) said: "It will be written against him." The man said, "Then he has sought forgiveness and repented." The Prophet (ﷺ) said: "He will be forgiven and his repentance accepted." The man said: "Then he returns to committing a sin." The Prophet (ﷺ) said: "It will be written against him." The man said: "Then he has sought forgiveness and repented." The Prophet (ﷺ) said: "He will be forgiven and his repentance accepted. Allah will not tire of forgiveness unless you are tired of asking." (*al-Muʿjam al-Awsaṭ* 8918, *Ṣaḥīḥ* according to Ibn Ḥajar)

Abū Saʿīd al-Khudrī (رضي الله عنه) reported: The Messenger of Allah (ﷺ) said:

إِنَّ الشَّيْطَانَ قَالَ وَعِزَّتِكَ يَا رَبِّ لَا أَبْرَحُ أُغْوِي عِبَادَكَ مَا دَامَتْ أَرْوَاحُهُمْ فِي أَجْسَادِهِمْ قَالَ الرَّبُّ وَعِزَّتِي وَجَلَالِي لَا أَزَالُ أَغْفِرُ لَهُمْ مَا اسْتَغْفَرُونِي

"*Shayṭān* said: 'By Your might, O Lord, I will continue to mislead the children of Adam, as long as their souls are in their bodies.' The Lord said: 'By My might and majesty, I will continue to forgive them, as long as they seek My forgiveness.' " (*Musnad Aḥmad* 27627, *Ṣaḥīḥ*)

g. *Allah is most delighted at his servant's repentance*

Anas (رضي الله عنه) reported: The Messenger of Allah (ﷺ) said:

لَلَّهُ أَشَدُّ فَرَحًا بِتَوْبَةِ عَبْدِهِ حِينَ يَتُوبُ إِلَيْهِ مِنْ أَحَدِكُمْ كَانَ عَلَى رَاحِلَتِهِ بِأَرْضِ فَلَاةٍ فَانْفَلَتَتْ مِنْهُ وَعَلَيْهَا طَعَامُهُ وَشَرَابُهُ فَأَيِسَ مِنْهَا فَأَتَى شَجَرَةً فَاضْطَجَعَ فِي ظِلِّهَا قَدْ أَيِسَ مِنْ رَاحِلَتِهِ فَبَيْنَا هُوَ كَذَلِكَ إِذَا هُوَ بِهَا قَائِمَةً عِنْدَهُ فَأَخَذَ بِخِطَامِهَا ثُمَّ قَالَ مِنْ شِدَّةِ الْفَرَحِ اللَّهُمَّ أَنْتَ عَبْدِي وَأَنَا رَبُّكَ أَخْطَأَ مِنْ شِدَّةِ الْفَرَحِ

"Allah is more delighted at the repentance of His servant than one of you who lost his riding animal on a journey in a barren land while it carries his food and drink. He loses all hope as he comes to a tree to lie down in its shade, despairing over his animal, but suddenly he finds it standing over him. He takes hold of its reins and then he greatly rejoices, saying: 'O Allah, You are my servant and I am your Lord!' He makes a mistake due to his great joy." (*Ṣaḥīḥ Muslim* 2747)

h. ***Reward for each believer he seeks forgiveness for***

ʿUbādah ibn al-Ṣāmit (رضي الله عنه) reported: The Messenger of Allah (ﷺ) said:

مَنِ اسْتَغْفَرَ لِلْمُؤْمِنِينَ وَالْمُؤْمِنَاتِ كَتَبَ اللَّهُ لَهُ بِكُلِّ مُؤْمِنٍ وَمُؤْمِنَةٍ حَسَنَةً

"Whoever seeks forgiveness for the believing men and women, Allah will record a good deed for him for each man and woman." (*Musnad al-Shāmīyyīn* 2118, *Jayyid* (good) according to al-Haythamī)

i. ***Allah forgives even if your sins pile up to the skies***

Abū Hurayrah (رضي الله عنه) reported: The Prophet (ﷺ) said:

لَوْ أَخْطَأْتُمْ حَتَّى تَبْلُغَ خَطَايَاكُمُ السَّمَاءَ ثُمَّ تُبْتُمْ لَتَابَ عَلَيْكُمْ

"If your sins were to reach to the heavens and then you repented, Allah would still accept your repentance." (*Sunan Ibn Mājah* 4248, *Ṣaḥīḥ* according to al-Albānī)

Anas ibn Mālik (رضي الله عنه) reported: The Messenger of Allah (ﷺ) said:

قَالَ اللَّهُ تَبَارَكَ وَتَعَالَى يَا ابْنَ آدَمَ إِنَّكَ مَا دَعَوْتَنِي وَرَجَوْتَنِي غَفَرْتُ لَكَ عَلَى مَا كَانَ فِيكَ وَلَا أُبَالِي يَا ابْنَ آدَمَ لَوْ بَلَغَتْ ذُنُوبُكَ عَنَانَ السَّمَاءِ ثُمَّ اسْتَغْفَرْتَنِي غَفَرْتُ لَكَ وَلَا أُبَالِي يَا ابْنَ آدَمَ إِنَّكَ لَوْ أَتَيْتَنِي بِقُرَابِ الْأَرْضِ خَطَايَا ثُمَّ لَقِيتَنِي لَا تُشْرِكُ بِي شَيْئًا لَأَتَيْتُكَ بِقُرَابِهَا مَغْفِرَةً

"Allah the Almighty said: 'O son of Adam, if you call upon Me and place your hope in Me, I will forgive you without hesitation. O son of Adam, if you have sins piling up to the clouds and then ask for My forgiveness, I will forgive you without hesitation. O son of Adam, if you come to Me with enough sins to fill the earth and then you meet Me without associating anything with Me, I will come to you with enough forgiveness to fill the earth.' " (*Sunan al-Tirmidhī* 3540, *Ṣaḥīḥ*)

j. Regret is part of repentance

ʿAbdullāh ibn Masʿūd (ﷺ) reported: The Messenger of Allah (ﷺ) said:

النَّدَمُ تَوْبَةٌ

"Regret is part of repentance." (*Sunan Ibn Mājah* 4252, *Ṣaḥīḥ* according to Al-Albānī)

k. Allah accepts repentance day and night

Abū Mūsā (ﷺ) reported: The Prophet (ﷺ) said:

إِنَّ اللَّهَ عَزَّ وَجَلَّ يَبْسُطُ يَدَهُ بِاللَّيْلِ لِيَتُوبَ مُسِيءُ النَّهَارِ وَيَبْسُطُ يَدَهُ بِالنَّهَارِ لِيَتُوبَ مُسِيءُ اللَّيْلِ حَتَّى تَطْلُعَ الشَّمْسُ مِنْ مَغْرِبِهَا

"Verily, Allah the Almighty stretches out His hand by night to accept the repentance of those who sin by day, and He stretches out His hand by day to accept the repentance of those who sin by night, until the sun rises from the west." (*Ṣaḥīḥ Muslim* 2759)

l. Whoever has Iman will eventually enter Jannah

Abū Dharr (ﷺ) reported: The Messenger of Allah (ﷺ) said:

أَتَانِي جِبْرِيلُ عَلَيْهِ السَّلَام فَبَشَّرَنِي أَنَّهُ مَنْ مَاتَ مِنْ أُمَّتِكَ لَا يُشْرِكُ بِاللَّهِ شَيْئًا دَخَلَ الْجَنَّةَ قُلْتُ وَإِنْ زَنَى وَإِنْ سَرَقَ قَالَ وَإِنْ زَنَى وَإِنْ سَرَقَ

"Jibrīl (ﷺ) came to me to give the good news that anyone from my nation who dies without associating partners with Allah will enter *Jannah*." I said: "Even if he commits adultery and theft?" The Prophet (ﷺ) said: "Even if he commits adultery and theft." (*Ṣaḥīḥ al-Bukhārī* 1237, *Ṣaḥīḥ Muslim* 94)

Al-Nawawī (ﷺ) said:

فَهُوَ حُجَّةٌ لِمَذْهَبِ أَهْلِ السُّنَّةِ أَنَّ أَصْحَابَ الْكَبَائِرِ لَا يُقْطَعُ لَهُمْ بِالنَّارِ وَأَنَّهُمْ إِنْ دَخَلُوهَا أُخْرِجُوا مِنْهَا وَخُتِمَ لَهُمْ بِالْخُلُودِ فِي الْجَنَّةِ

"This [*ḥadīth*] is proof for the People of the Sunnah, that those who commit major sins will not remain in *Jahannam* forever. They will be taken out if they enter *Jahannam* and eventually admitted into *Jannah*." (*Sharḥ al-Nawawī ʿalā Ṣaḥīḥ Muslim* 94)

m. ***Allah runs to the one who walks to Him***

Abū Hurayrah (ﷺ) reported: The Messenger of Allah (ﷺ) said:

يَقُولُ اللَّهُ تَعَالَى أَنَا عِنْدَ ظَنِّ عَبْدِي بِي وَأَنَا مَعَهُ إِذَا ذَكَرَنِي فَإِنْ ذَكَرَنِي فِي نَفْسِهِ ذَكَرْتُهُ فِي نَفْسِي وَإِنْ ذَكَرَنِي فِي مَلَإٍ ذَكَرْتُهُ فِي مَلَإٍ خَيْرٍ مِنْهُمْ وَإِنْ تَقَرَّبَ إِلَيَّ بِشِبْرٍ تَقَرَّبْتُ إِلَيْهِ ذِرَاعًا وَإِنْ تَقَرَّبَ إِلَيَّ ذِرَاعًا تَقَرَّبْتُ إِلَيْهِ بَاعًا وَإِنْ أَتَانِي يَمْشِي أَتَيْتُهُ هَرْوَلَةً

"Allah the Almighty says: 'I am as My servant expects Me and I am with him as he remembers Me. If he remembers Me in himself, I will remember him in Myself. If he mentions Me in a gathering, I will mention him in a greater gathering. When he draws near Me by the span of his hand, I draw near him by the length of a cubit. When he draws near Me by the length of a cubit, I draw near him by the length of a fathom. When he comes to Me walking, I come to him running.' " (*Ṣaḥīḥ al-Bukhārī* 6970, *Ṣaḥīḥ Muslim* 2675)

n. ***The Duʿā of Repentance (Sayyid al-Istighfār) that will take you to Jannah***

Shaddād ibn Aws (ﷺ) reported: The Prophet (ﷺ) said to him:

"The best way to seek forgiveness is that you say:

اللَّهُمَّ أَنْتَ رَبِّي لَا إِلَهَ إِلَّا أَنْتَ خَلَقْتَنِي وَأَنَا عَبْدُكَ وَأَنَا عَلَى عَهْدِكَ وَوَعْدِكَ مَا اسْتَطَعْتُ أَعُوذُ

بِكَ مِنْ شَرِّ مَا صَنَعْتُ أَبُوءُ لَكَ بِنِعْمَتِكَ عَلَيَّ وَأَبُوءُ لَكَ بِذَنْبِي فَاغْفِرْ لِي فَإِنَّهُ لَا يَغْفِرُ الذُّنُوبَ إِلَّا أَنْتَ

'O Allah, You are my Lord. There is no god but You. You created me and I am Your servant, I am committed to You and Your promise, as much as I can. I seek refuge in You from the evil I have done. I acknowledge Your favors and I acknowledge my sins, so forgive me. Verily, no one forgives sins but You.' "

The Prophet (ﷺ) said:

وَمَنْ قَالَهَا مِنْ النَّهَارِ مُوقِنًا بِهَا فَمَاتَ مِنْ يَوْمِهِ قَبْلَ أَنْ يُمْسِيَ فَهُوَ مِنْ أَهْلِ الْجَنَّةِ وَمَنْ قَالَهَا مِنْ اللَّيْلِ وَهُوَ مُوقِنٌ بِهَا فَمَاتَ قَبْلَ أَنْ يُصْبِحَ فَهُوَ مِنْ أَهْلِ الْجَنَّةِ

"Whoever says this in the day with conviction and dies before evening, he will be among the people of *Jannah*. Whoever says this in the night with conviction and dies before morning, he will be among the people of *Jannah*." (*Ṣaḥīḥ al-Bukhārī* 6306)

o. *Allah will forgive you even if you fled from the battlefield*

Zayd ibn Ḥārithah (رضي الله عنه) reported: The Messenger of Allah (ﷺ) said:

مَنْ قَالَ أَسْتَغْفِرُ اللَّهَ الْعَظِيمَ الَّذِي لَا إِلَهَ إِلَّا هُوَ الْحَيَّ الْقَيُّومَ وَأَتُوبُ إِلَيْهِ غُفِرَ لَهُ وَإِنْ كَانَ فَرَّ مِنْ الزَّحْفِ

"Whoever says this supplication: 'I seek forgiveness from Allah the Almighty, besides whom there is no god, the Living, the Sustainer, and I repent to him' then Allah will forgive him even if he fled from battle." (*Sunan al-Tirmidhī* 3577, *Ṣaḥīḥ*)

Bāb at-Tawbah, where hearts find rebirth,
In the light of repentance, they reclaim their worth.

He enters Paradise, remembering his sins,
In humility, a new chapter begins.

Allah's love for repentance, boundless and wide,
In *Jannah*'s gardens, His mercy will guide.

Prophets and righteous, their hearts pure and clean,
In Paradise's beauty, their souls shall convene.

Allah laughs for two types, it's said,
In *Jannah*'s joy, their souls are led.

Blessed is the seeker of forgiveness' grace,
In *Jannah*'s bliss, they'll find their rightful place.

Allah's utmost joy, a servant's return,
In repentance's light, their souls truly yearn.

For every believer, forgiveness they seek,
In *Jannah*'s embrace, they'll find what they seek.

Though sins pile up, as high as the skies,
Allah's mercy flows, a boundless surprise.

Regret, a part of repentance's plea,
In *Jannah*'s radiance, they'll find eternity.

Day and night, Allah's grace does abide,
In *Jannah*'s light, the penitent will confide.

With the flame of faith, *Jannah* they'll eventually earn,
In Allah's love, their souls shall forever discern.

Allah rushes to meet, as one walks His way,
In *Jannah*'s glory, they'll eternally stay.

The *Duʿā* of Repentance, *Sayyid al-Istighfār*,
A path to *Jannah*, where the faithful go far.

Even if one fled from the battlefield's sight,
Allah's mercy, for the sorry, sets things right.

CHAPTER

Eleven

BĀB AL-ḤAJJ

GATE OF HAJJ[8]

8 According to Ibn Ḥajar al-ʿAsqalānī (رحمه الله). He says that the sound *ḥadīth* mentioned four names of the Gates of *Jannah*; so there is no doubt there will be a gate with the name *al-Ḥajj* since it is one of the fundamentals of *Islām*. There are other names mentioned in different *aḥādīth*.

Those who are known to always perform the Hajj will be admitted through this door.

وَإِذْ جَعَلْنَا ٱلْبَيْتَ مَثَابَةً لِّلنَّاسِ وَأَمْنًا وَٱتَّخِذُوا۟ مِن مَّقَامِ إِبْرَٰهِـۧمَ مُصَلًّى ۖ وَعَهِدْنَآ إِلَىٰٓ إِبْرَٰهِـۧمَ وَإِسْمَـٰعِيلَ أَن طَهِّرَا بَيْتِىَ لِلطَّآئِفِينَ وَٱلْعَـٰكِفِينَ وَٱلرُّكَّعِ ٱلسُّجُودِ ﴿١٢٥﴾

"And [mention] when We made the House (i.e., the Kaʿbah) a place of return for the people and [a place of] security. And take, [O believers], from the standing place of Ibrāhīm a place of prayer. And We charged Ibrāhīm and Ismāʿīl, [saying]: 'Purify My House for those who perform *ṭawāf* and those who are staying [there] for worship and those who bow and prostrate [in prayer].' " (*al-Baqarah*, 2:125)

وَأَذِّن فِى ٱلنَّاسِ بِٱلْحَجِّ يَأْتُوكَ رِجَالًا وَعَلَىٰ كُلِّ ضَامِرٍ يَأْتِينَ مِن كُلِّ فَجٍّ عَمِيقٍ ﴿٢٧﴾

"And proclaim to the people the Hajj [pilgrimage]; they will come to you on foot and on every lean camel; they will come from every distant pass." (*al-Ḥajj*, 22:27)

a. *Hajj brings you out of darkness*

ʿAbdur Raḥmān ibn Samurah (﷠) reported: The Messenger of Allah (ﷺ) came out to us and he said: "Verily, I saw something wondrous last night... I saw a man of my nation with darkness before him, darkness behind him, darkness to his right, darkness to his left, darkness above him, and darkness below him, and his pilgrimages came to bring him out of darkness..." (*al-Muʿjam al-Kabīr* 39, *Ṣaḥīḥ li-ghayrihī* (authentic due to external evidence), according to Ibn Taymiyyah)

b. *Faith, jihad, and Hajj are better than all other deeds*

Māʿiz al-Tamīmī (ﷺ) reported: The Prophet (ﷺ) was asked: "Which deeds are best?" The Prophet (ﷺ) said:

الْإِيمَانُ بِاللهِ وَحْدَهُ ثُمَّ الْجِهَادُ ثُمَّ حَجَّةٌ بَرَّةٌ تَفْضُلُ سَائِرَ الْعَمَلِ كَمَا بَيْنَ مَطْلِعِ الشَّمْسِ إِلَى مَغْرِبِهَا

"Faith in Allah alone, then jihad, then a blessed pilgrimage are better than all other deeds like the distance between the rising of the sun and its setting." (*al-Muʿjam al-Kabīr* 17227, *Ṣaḥīḥ* according to al-Albānī)

c. *Three are guaranteed Jannah from Allah*

Abū Hurayrah (ﷺ) reported: The Messenger of Allah (ﷺ) said:

ثَلاثَةٌ فِي ضَمَانِ اللَّهِ عَزَّ وَجَلَّ رَجُلٌ خَرَجَ مِنْ بَيْتِهِ إِلَى مَسْجِدٍ مِنْ مَسَاجِدِ اللَّهِ عَزَّ وَجَلَّ وَرَجُلٌ خَرَجَ غَازِيًا فِي سَبِيلِ اللَّهِ عَزَّ وَجَلَّ وَرَجُلٌ خَرَجَ حَاجًّا

"Three people have a guarantee from Allah the Almighty: a man who leaves his house to attend one of the mosques of Allah the Almighty; a man who goes out waging a campaign in the way of Allah the Almighty; and a man who goes out for the *Hajj* pilgrimage." (*Musnad al-Ḥumaydī* 1041, *Ṣaḥīḥ* according to al-Arnāʾūṭ)

d. *Hajj erases all sins before it*

ʿAmr ibn al-ʿĀṣ (ﷺ) reported: The Prophet (ﷺ) said:

أَمَا عَلِمْتَ أَنَّ الْإِسْلَامَ يَهْدِمُ مَا كَانَ قَبْلَهُ وَأَنَّ الْهِجْرَةَ تَهْدِمُ مَا كَانَ قَبْلَهَا وَأَنَّ الْحَجَّ يَهْدِمُ مَا كَانَ قَبْلَهُ

"Do you not know that embracing *Islām* wipes away all sins committed before it, that emigration wipes away what came before it, and the Hajj pilgrimage wipes away what came before it?" (*Ṣaḥīḥ Muslim* 121)

e. *When someone dies performing Hajj*

Ibn ʿAbbās (ﷺ) reported:

A man performing the pilgrimage was thrown from his camel and died while we were with the Prophet (ﷺ). The Prophet (ﷺ) said:

اغْسِلُوهُ بِمَاءٍ وَسِدْرٍ وَكَفِّنُوهُ فِي ثَوْبَيْنِ وَلَا تُمِسُّوهُ طِيبًا وَلَا تُخَمِّرُوا رَأْسَهُ فَإِنَّ اللَّهَ يَبْعَثُهُ يَوْمَ الْقِيَامَةِ مُلَبِّيًا

"Wash him with water mixed with the leaves of a lote (*Sidr*) tree and shroud him in his two garments. Do not perfume him and do not cover his head, for Allah will raise him on the Day of Resurrection performing the call of the pilgrimage (*talbiyah*)." (*Ṣaḥīḥ al-Bukhārī* 1208, *Ṣaḥīḥ Muslim* 1206)

Abū Hurayrah (ﷺ) reported: The Messenger of Allah (ﷺ) said:

مَنْ خَرَجَ حَاجًّا فَمَاتَ كُتِبَ لَهُ أَجْرُ الْحَاجِّ إِلَى يَوْمِ الْقِيَامَةِ وَمَنْ خَرَجَ مُعْتَمِرًا فَمَاتَ كُتِبَ لَهُ أَجْرُ الْمُعْتَمِرِ إِلَى يَوْمِ الْقِيَامَةِ وَمَنْ خَرَجَ غَازِيًا فَمَاتَ كُتِبَ لَهُ أَجْرُ الْغَازِي إِلَى يَوْمِ الْقِيَامَةِ

"Whoever goes out for the Hajj pilgrimage and dies, the reward of Hajj will be written for him until the Day of Resurrection. Whoever goes out for the ʿ*umrah* pilgrimage and dies, the reward of ʿ*umrah* will be written for him until the Day of Resurrection. Whoever goes out for military service and dies, the reward of military service will be written for him until the Day of Resurrection." (*al-Muʿjam al-Awsaṭ* 5467, *Ṣaḥīḥ li-ghayrihī* (authentic due to external evidence), according to al-Albānī)

f. Allah frees His servants on the Day of ʿArafah

ʿĀʾishah (۝) reported: The Messenger of Allah (۝) said:

مَا مِنْ يَوْمٍ أَكْثَرَ مِنْ أَنْ يُعْتِقَ اللَّهُ فِيهِ عَبْدًا مِنْ النَّارِ مِنْ يَوْمِ عَرَفَةَ وَإِنَّهُ لَيَدْنُو ثُمَّ يُبَاهِي بِهِمْ الْمَلَائِكَةَ فَيَقُولُ مَا أَرَادَ هَؤُلَاءِ

"There is no day upon which Allah frees more of His servants from *Jahannam* than the Day of ʿArafah. He draws near and then He boasts of them to the angels, saying: 'What do these servants want?'" (*Ṣaḥīḥ Muslim* 1348)

ʿAbdullāh ibn ʿAmr (۝) reported: The Prophet (۝) said:

إِنَّ اللَّهَ عَزَّ وَجَلَّ يُبَاهِي مَلَائِكَتَهُ عَشِيَّةَ عَرَفَةَ بِأَهْلِ عَرَفَةَ فَيَقُولُ انْظُرُوا إِلَى عِبَادِي أَتَوْنِي شُعْثًا غُبْرًا

"Verily, Allah the Almighty boasts to His angels of the pilgrims on the afternoon of the Day of ʿArafah, saying: 'Look at My servants, coming to Me disheveled and dusty.'" (*Musnad Aḥmad* 7089, *Ṣaḥīḥ* according to Aḥmad Shākir)

g. Best jihad for women is accepted Hajj

ʿĀʾishah (۝) reported: I said: "O Messenger of Allah, shall we not attend the expeditions and fight in jihad alongside you?" The Prophet (۝) said:

لَكِنَّ أَحْسَنَ الْجِهَادِ وَأَجْمَلَهُ الْحَجُّ حَجٌّ مَبْرُورٌ

"No, rather the best and most beautiful jihad for you is the Hajj, a righteous pilgrimage." (*Ṣaḥīḥ al-Bukhārī* 1762)

h. Reward for Hajj is Jannah

Abū Hurayrah (⁕) reported that the Prophet (⁕) said:

الْحَجُّ الْمَبْرُورُ لَيْسَ لَهُ جَزَاءٌ إِلَّا الْجَنَّةُ

"The reward for a *Ḥajj Mabrūr* is nothing but *Jannah*." (*Ṣaḥīḥ al-Bukhārī* 1773, and *Ṣaḥīḥ Muslim* 1349)

'Abdullāh ibn 'Umar (⁕) reported: The Messenger of Allah (⁕) said:

مَنْ طَافَ أُسْبُوعًا يُحْصِيهِ وَصَلَّى رَكْعَتَيْنِ كَانَ لَهُ كَعِدْلِ رَقَبَةٍ مَا رَفَعَ رَجُلٌ قَدَمًا وَلَا وَضَعَهَا إِلَّا كُتِبَتْ لَهُ عَشْرُ حَسَنَاتٍ وَحُطَّ عَنْهُ عَشْرُ سَيِّئَاتٍ وَرُفِعَ لَهُ عَشْرُ دَرَجَاتٍ

"Whoever circles the *Ka'bah* seven times and prays two cycles will be rewarded as if he had freed a slave. A man does not raise his foot, nor bring it back down, but that ten good deeds will be written for him, ten bad deeds will be erased, and he will be raised by ten degrees (in *Jannah*)." (*Musnad Aḥmad* 4462, *Ḥasan* according to al-Arnā'ūṭ)

i. Hajj purifies a person from sins and removes poverty

'Abdullāh ibn Mas'ūd (⁕) reported: The Messenger of Allah (⁕) said:

تَابِعُوا بَيْنَ الْحَجِّ وَالْعُمْرَةِ فَإِنَّهُمَا يَنْفِيَانِ الْفَقْرَ وَالذُّنُوبَ كَمَا يَنْفِي الْكِيرُ خَبَثَ الْحَدِيدِ وَالذَّهَبِ وَالْفِضَّةِ وَلَيْسَ لِلْحَجَّةِ الْمَبْرُورَةِ ثَوَابٌ إِلَّا الْجَنَّةُ

"Perform the Hajj and 'umrah pilgrimages, one after another, for they both erase poverty and sins just as the furnace removes impurity from iron, gold, and silver. There is no reward for a *Ḥajj Mabrūr* but *Jannah*." (*Sunan al-Tirmidhī* 810, *Ṣaḥīḥ*)

j. *ʿUmrah in Ramaḍān is equal to the reward of Hajj*

Ibn ʿAbbās (ﷺ) reported: The Prophet (ﷺ) said:

إِنَّ عُمْرَةً فِي رَمَضَانَ حَجَّةٌ

"Verily, the *ʿumrah* pilgrimage during *Ramaḍān* is equal to that of Hajj." (*Ṣaḥīḥ al-Bukhārī* 1782, *Ṣaḥīḥ Muslim* 1256)

k. *Saying the talbiyah is glad tidings of Jannah*

Abū Hurayrah (ﷺ) reported: The Prophet (ﷺ) said:

مَا أَهَلَّ مُهِلٌّ قَطُّ إِلا بُشِّرَ وَلا كَبَّرَ مُكَبِّرٌ قَطُّ إِلا بُشِّرَ قِيلَ يَا رَسُولَ اللَّهِ بِالْجَنَّةِ قَالَ نَعَمْ

"A pilgrim never raises his voice answering the call to Allah but that he is given glad tidings, and a pilgrim never raises his voice in exalting Allah but that he is given glad tidings." It was said: "O Messenger of Allah, of *Jannah*?" The Prophet (ﷺ) said: "Yes." (*al-Muʿjam al-Kabīr* 7987, *Ḥasan* according to al-Albānī)

l. *Whoever performs Hajj or ʿumrah is the guest of Allah*

Jābir (ﷺ) reported: The Messenger of Allah (ﷺ) said:

الْحُجَّاجُ وَالْعُمَّارُ وَفْدُ اللَّهِ دَعَاهُمْ فَأَجَابُوهُ وَسَأَلُوهُ فَأَعْطَاهُمْ

"The pilgrims of Hajj and *ʿumrah* are the guests of Allah. He called them and they answered Him. They ask from Him and He gives them." (*Kashf al-Astār* 1075, *Ḥasan* according to al-Albānī)

m. Leaving for the masjid will reward you with Hajj

Abū Umāmah (رضي الله عنه) reported: The Prophet (ﷺ) said:

مَنْ غَدَا إِلَى الْمَسْجِدِ لَا يُرِيدُ إِلَّا أَنْ يَتَعَلَّمَ خَيْرًا أَوْ يَعْلَمَهُ كَانَ لَهُ كَأَجْرِ حَاجٍّ تَامًّا حَجَّتُهُ

"Whoever leaves for the *masjid* in the morning, for no reason but to learn goodness or teach others, he will have a reward as if he has completed the Hajj pilgrimage." (*al-Muʿjam al-Kabīr* 7346, Ṣaḥīḥ according to al-Albānī)

Bāb al-Ḥajj, a gate of sacred light,
From darkness to the holy, it guides the flight.

Faith, jihad, Hajj, the deeds that truly shine,
In Allah's favour, their souls align.

Three, guaranteed by Allah's decree,
In *Jannah*'s grace, they'll eternally be.

Hajj erases sins, a pure soul's creed,
In *Jannah*'s gardens, their hearts are freed.

When one dies on Hajj, a blessed way,
In Allah's love, they find their eternal day.

On ʿArafāt's day, Allah's servants are set free,
In *Jannah*'s bliss, their souls will forever be.

For women, Hajj is the best jihad,
In Allah's mercy, they will ever be glad.

Jannah's reward, for those who embark,
Hajj's journey, a blessed spark.

Purifying souls, removing life's weight,
In *Jannah*'s gardens, they'll find their fate.

ʿUmrah in *Ramaḍān*, like Hajj's sweet call,
In Allah's love, they'll all stand tall.

Saying the *talbiyah*, glad tidings from above,
In *Jannah*'s beauty, they find their love.

Hajj's pilgrims, Allah's honoured guests,
In Paradise's grace, they are truly blessed.

Leaving for the *masjid*, a righteous way,
In Hajj's blessings, their hearts will sway.

Conclusion

O seeker of the gates, with knowledge in your hand,
Let narrations light your path, like grains of golden sand.

For each gate of *Jannah*, a noble goal to chase,
With deeds and faith combined, in Allah's loving grace.

Let not these words remain as mere tales of old,
But urges to action, let your heart unfold.

Work hard to gain entry through every gate you see,
In Allah's mercy, your soul forever free.

So heed these narrations, let them light your way,
With striving and devotion, let your heart obey.

For in the garden of *Jannah*, your soul shall thrive,
Through every gate of Paradise, your faith alive.

Let knowledge be your compass, your actions be your key,
To unlock all the gates, in *Jannah*'s beauty to be.

With faith as your guide, and actions pure and true,
May all the Gates of *Jannah* open wide for you!